Cultural Policy and East Asian Rivalry

Asian Cultural Studies: Transnational and Dialogic Approaches

The series advances transnational intellectual dialogue over diverse issues that are shared in various Asian countries and cities.

Series Editor:

Koichi Iwabuchi, Professor of Media and Cultural Studies and Director of Monash Asia Institute, Monash University, Australia

Editorial Collective:

Ien Ang (University of Western Sydney)
Chris Berry (King's College London)
John Erni (Hong Kong Baptist University)
Daniel Goh (National University of Singapore)
Ariel Heryanto (Australian National University)
Kim Hyun Mee (Yonsei University)

Titles in the Series:

Cultural Policy and East Asian Rivalry

The Hong Kong Gaming Industry

Anthony Y. H. Fung

ROWMAN & LITTLEFIELD
INTERNATIONAL

London • New York

Published by Rowman & Littlefield International, Ltd.
Unit A, Whitacre Mews, 26-34 Stannary Street, London SE11 4AB
www.rowmaninternational.com

Rowman & Littlefield International, Ltd., is an affiliate of Rowman & Littlefield
4501 Forbes Boulevard, Suite 200, Lanham, Maryland 20706, USA
With additional offices in Boulder, New York, Toronto (Canada), and London (UK)
www.rowman.com

British Library Cataloguing is available from the British Library

ISBN: HB 978-1-78348-624-3
ISBN: PB 978-1-78348-625-0

Library of Congress Cataloging-in-Publication Data

Names: Fung, Anthony Y. H., author.
Title: Cultural policy and East Asian rivalry : the Hong Kong gaming industry
   / Anthony Fung.
Description: Lanham : Rowman & Littlefield International, [2018] | Series:
   Asian cultural studies: transnational and dialogic approaches | Includes
   bibliographical references and index.
Identifiers: LCCN 2017060147 (print) | LCCN 2018010768 (ebook) | ISBN
   9781783486267 (Electronic) | ISBN 9781783486243 (cloth : alk. paper) |
   ISBN 9781783486250 (pbk. : alk. paper)
Subjects: LCSH: Electronic games industry--China--Hong Kong. |
   China--Cultural policy. | East Asia--Cultural policy.
Classification: LCC HD9993.E453 (ebook) | LCC HD9993.E453 C464 2018 (print) |
   DDC 338.4/77948095125--dc23
LC record available at https://lccn.loc.gov/2017060147

Contents

List of Figures

List of Tables

List of Abbreviations

ACGHK	Animation-Comic-Game Hong Kong
AEC	ASEAN Economic Community
ANI-COM	Animation-Comic-Game Hong Kong
ARPU	Average revenue per user
ASEA	Annual Survey of Economic Activities (Hong Kong)
ASEAN	Association of Southeast Asian Nations
BECR	Bureau for External Cultural Relations (China)
CAA	Consumer Affairs Agency (Japan)
CCO	China Copyright Office
CEPA	China and Hong Kong Closer Economic Partnership Agreement
CityU	City University of Hong Kong
CMM	Capacity maturity model
CMMI	Capacity maturity model integration
CreateHK	Create Hong Kong
CUHK	Chinese University of Hong Kong
DCI	Department of Cultural Industry (China)
DCMA	Department of Cultural Market Administration (China)
DCMS	Department of Culture, Media and Sport (United Kingdom)
DIGRA	Digital Games Research Association
EMA	Content Evaluation and Monitoring Association (Japan)

ESRB	Entertainment Software Rating Board
GAPP	General Administration of Press and Publication (China)
GDP	Gross domestic product
HKBN	Hong Kong Broadband Network
HKD	Hong Kong dollars
HKGIA	Hong Kong Game Industry Association
IBM	International Business Machines
ICT	Information and communication technology
IDC	International Data Corporation
IFPI	International Federation of Phonographic Industry
IGA	Online in-game advertising
IGE	International gaming and entertainment
IT	Information technology
JOGA	Japan Online Game Association
HKSAR	Hong Kong Special Administrative Region
KGDPI	Korea Game Development and Promotion Institute
KGIA	Korea Game Industry Agency
KGPC	Korea Game Promotion Centre
KOCCA	Korea Creative Content Agency
KOSDAQ	Korean Securities Dealers Automated Quotations
MII	Ministry of Information Industry (China)
MCT	Ministry of Culture and Tourism (Korea)
METI	Ministry of Economy, Trade, and Industry (Japan)
MMORPG	Massively multiplayer online role-playing game
MOC	Ministry of Culture (China)
MTR	Mass Transit Railway (Hong Kong)
MUD	Multiple user dialogue
MUG	Multiple user graphic
NGO	Nongovernmental organization
NTD	New Taiwan Dollars
OECD	Organization for Economic Cooperation and Development
PC	Personal computer

PK	Player kill
PEGI	Pan European Game Information
PLA	People's Liberation Army (China)
PolyU	Hong Kong Polytechnic University
PRC	People's Republic of China
RMT	Real money trade
RPG	Role-playing games
SAPPRFT	State Administration of Press, Publication, Radio, Film and Television (China)
SARFT	State Administration of Radio, Film, and Television (China)
SCGIM	Software, computer games, and interactive media
SNS	Social networking services
SPPR	Strategic Public Policy Research (Hong Kong)
STG	Shooting games
THAAD	Terminal high-altitude area defense
UE	User experience
UNESCO	United Nations Educational, Scientific and Cultural Organization

Acknowledgments

In modern history, Hong Kong's geocultural significance has been based on its alliances and rivalries, its connections and competition, and its estrangement from and ties to neighboring cities and nations, all of which apply to the development of its creative industries. During the Cultural Revolution, Hong Kong served as a window for China's cultural exchanges. When television entered Hong Kong households in the 1970s, children were fed Japanese anime. In the 1980s, Japanese melodies exported to Hong Kong gave rise to Cantopop, much of which was Japanese ballads dubbed with local lyrics. The export of movies and pop music from Hong Kong to China led to new forms of entertainment after China opened its market in the 1990s. In 2000, the Korean wave began to dominate Hong Kong's popular culture. Hence the question is raised. Will the current rise of China as the largest global game-developer eliminate Hong Kong's role in the East Asian region? Will the state-driven cultural policies of South Korea and China affect Hong Kong's laissez-faire approach to its creative industries?

This book examines Hong Kong's game industry vis-à-vis the game industries in the East Asian region and considers the possible expansion of Hong Kong's game industry through its ties with China and the encroachment in the local game market of East Asian game companies.

Although my research interest led me to explore this cultural phenomenon, I also have a personal interest in games and gaming. I sometimes reminisce about my school days in Minnesota when it was thirty degrees below zero outside. Although personal computers had not yet become popular, I often buried myself in the computer room, playing computer games when I was supposed to be studying. I wanted to understand the immeasurable charm and fatal attraction of games and how they were created and marketed to me as well as others. This book extends this intellectual curiosity and summarizes my various studies on games and game interests in previous decades.

The initial funding for this project was provided by the Strategic Public Research Grant Market of the Research Grant Council in the Hong Kong Special Administrative Region (Project no. 4001-SPPR-09). This source also funded "Mapping the Hong Kong game industry: Cultural policy, creative clusters, and the Asian market," for which I was a chief investigator at the Chinese University of Hong Kong. In my position as a professor in the Global Talent Scheme of China in the School of Art and Communication at Beijing Normal University, I was able to conduct extensive research on Chinese cultural policy and creative industries.

However, I emphasize that I have not been alone on my journey of game research. I have been fortunate to work on various subprojects with a group of dedicated international scholars. John Erni worked with me in Hong Kong. Matthew Chew, Peichi Chung, and I collaborated on fieldwork in China and Southeast Asia. Mirko Ernkvist brought me to Japan to deepen my understanding of the game scene in that country. Michael Keane, John Banks, and Darryl Woodford opened my eyes to the Australian and North American game industries. Jeroen de Kloet and David Nieborg were my partners in researching the European game industry. We became not only good research teammates but also good friends. I would like to express my heartfelt gratitude to all my coresearchers throughout the years.

For the fieldwork in Hong Kong, I would like to thank the Hong Kong Game Industries Association. In particular, I want to thank Mr. Sze Yan Ngai and Mrs. Sze, who helped me conduct local fieldwork. I would also like to express my respect for all the professionals in the Hong Kong gaming industries. I thank Iris Guan and Liu Yusu for helping me in my years of fieldwork by providing access to game companies and government officials in China. I thank Xie Yinghua for assisting in the interviews I conducted in South Korea. I am indebted to Daisy Cheng and Brian Yeung, who helped organize the huge amount of data that was collected. I also want to thank all my correspondents and interviewees in Hong Kong, China, South Korea, and Japan.

I must thank Koichi Iwabuchi, my friend and the editor of this series, for his valuable support that began with my conception of East Asian rivalry and resulted in the birth of this book. Without him, this book would not have been possible. I also thank my publisher, Rowman & Littlefield, and their friendly executives, including Martina O'Sullivan, Natalie Linh Bolderston, and Holly Tyler, who led me through the pangs of labor in giving birth to this book.

This book was conceived "accidentally." In the summer of 2017, because of a minor accident in Beijing, I had to rest at home for more than two months. Writing this book became a valuable pastime for me during this prolonged summer vacation. For this reason, I thank my family members, who took care of me daily, and my friends, who visited me almost every day during my recovery. All of you gave me the energy and momentum to finish this book.

Game research is not just my academic job and intellectual interest: game research is my passion. I sincerely hope that games and gaming will emerge as a central pillar of the creative industries of Hong Kong. I also look forward to seeing more game researchers in Hong Kong and in East Asia who will unveil for readers the cultural significance of a game scene and industry exemplified by the increasing number of exciting games produced in this region.

Chapter One

The Game Industry and Cultural Policy

BACKGROUND

In 2017, *King of Glory* became the first Chinese mobile game to top the number of sales on the iOS platform since 2014, the year that statistics were first compiled. The game was developed by Tencent, which also owns *League of Legends*, the most popular online game in history. In China today, 80 million players are active daily, which means that for every 7 Chinese, there is 1 player of online games. Based on historical heroic Chinese figures across dynasties, in addition to legendary Japanese and Greek warriors, the gameplay of *King of Glory* involves attacking another player or team to increase and accumulate the virtual currency and military power of either a single player or a team of game-mates. Ironically, the game's popularity has led to tragedies, many of which have been reported in the media. In Hangzhou, China, according to a media report in June, a thirteen-year-old jumped from the fourth floor of a building after being scolded by his father because of the amount of time he spent playing online games, particularly *King of Glory*. The boy's father was reported to have heard his son say, "Why wasn't I capable of flying? If I had known, I would have not jumped from that high." He claimed his son had thought he could fly because of playing the game (*Beijing News*, 2017).

In April of the same year, official media also reported that after forty hours of "combating" on *King of Glory*—except for ordering a carry-out meal—a seventeen-year-old boy in Guangzhou suffered an acute cerebral stroke and was admitted to Jinan University First Hospital (People.cn, 2017). In July, the online media (without sources) reported that an eleven-year-old girl had spent more than RMB¥100,000 on a stolen credit card to play the game (People.cn, 2017).

The credibility of sources notwithstanding, it is not easy to determine, at least in the Chinese community, the degree of public anxiety about addiction to gaming and the general negative impression made by gaming. Without warning, the most significant trio of official Chinese media—the official online People.cn, *China's Daily* (Chinese version), and the Xinhua News Agency—publicly censured gaming and its excessive use. The *People's Daily* even called gaming "digital opium" (Zhang, 2017).

I find that the word *schizophrenia* best characterizes this phenomenon. In the same year (2017), the Ministry of Culture of the People's Republic of China and Shanghai City organized the Chinese Comic and Animation Expo in which the gaming industry was applauded for its role in the strategic development of China and in the international collaboration of China in the gaming industry. Simply put, this event exemplified a contradiction between the development of the game industries as a cultural and creative industry and the potential negative effect of gaming on society. However, my impression is that when the monetary growth of China and other East Asian countries is the topic, praise of the development of the game industry gains the upper hand in any discourse on the effects of gaming.

DIGITAL GAMES AND EVERYDAY LIFE

Even with the public's cognizance of and outcry against the potentially negative effects of gaming, digital games have permeated our daily lives as a form of entertainment, education, work, and sport through different communication technologies and devices. In Hong Kong, there are over 600,000 active online gamers, and every teenager owns an average 2.7 handheld devices (for games). These figures exclude students who complete assignments through educational online games at school and adults who indulge in handheld and mobile games on public transport. The popularity of games is also demonstrated by the large number of visitors (an average of 650,000 since 2010) who every year swamp ANI-com, the most important animation, games, and comics festival in Hong Kong (ANI-com, 2015). This popularity has led to controversy about the negative effects of games on society. Local media often report the adverse social and psychological effects of games—particularly from their sexual, violent, and racialized content—including antisocial addiction, social conflict triggered by online disputes, and alienation from parents and peers.

Despite the popularity and social significance of games, very few studies have been conducted on the game industry in Hong Kong. For too long, scholars have seen games as marginal, peripheral, and frivolous. In fact, games today are one of the most dominant entertainment forms in developed and developing economies as well as one of the most lucrative creative industries in the world, in addition to being the most profitable information technology (IT) application worldwide. The Centre for Cultural Policy Research's baseline study of creative industries, which was commissioned by the Hong Kong government, devoted only a few paragraphs to games (Central Policy Unit, 2003). It was then followed by studies that were funded via public policy research grants to investigate these industries, such as the film industry (e.g., Chan, Fung, & Ng, 2009). This book mainly documents the findings collected by my research team and me in an academic and policy study under a Strategic Public Policy Research grant from the Hong Kong Special Administrative Region (HKSAR) to investigate the game industry and gamers in Hong Kong and Asian markets since 2010.

The game industry's economic significance also has been overlooked by policy makers and scholars. A conservative estimate of the market size of gaming in Hong Kong, according to a recent study of digital entertainment by Create Hong Kong (CreateHK), in which I was the main investigator (on behalf of the Chinese University of Hong Kong), put its value at over US$1 billion in 2017 (Hong Kong Digital Entertainment Industry, 2017). This amount far exceeds that of the sales of music albums and movie tickets in Hong Kong. Moreover, the estimated number of game-relevant companies (including the development, publishing, distribution, and retail sectors) in Hong Kong has reached 2,800, which also surpasses the number of film-related companies (figure based on my interviews with representative companies). Today there seems to be a cultural policy discourse regarding the development of local creative industries, including the game industry. Through CreateHK, the HKSAR allocates funding to support game-industry-related events although there is still no direct financial support in terms of investment and grants (e.g., through tariffs, tax breaks, or development funds as in other Asian countries). Eyeing the big Chinese market that is adjacent to Hong Kong, arrangements have been made under the China and Hong Kong Closer Economic Partnership Agreement (CEPA), although the effectiveness of the agreement is variable. The effects are evident in Hong Kong's film (i.e., coproductions) and service industries but not in the local game industries.

Nevertheless, it is a fact that the game industry is conducive to augmenting the economy of a nation or a city (Fung, 2016). During the past decade, business consultants and strategists have recognized that the game industry can drive economic growth. The report "The video game market in China: Moving online or DFC" (KPMG, 2007), which was updated in 2016 in intelligence reports on online gaming, is a clear example. The recent experiences of South Korea, Japan, and China provide insights into the game business. In South Korea, the annual game output was expected to reach US$10.04 billion in 2017 (Statista, 2016a), US$13.67 billion in Japan in 2017 (Statista, 2016b), and US$24.4 billion in China in 2016 (Newzoo,

2016). In South Korea, amid a Korean wave of popular culture that is prevalent worldwide, the export of Korean games has been much stronger in terms of market revenues than the exports of its globally vaunted film industry (Jin, 2010). In Japan, online consumption, which accounts for most social media gaming, constitutes 2.98 percent of the country's annual GDP (Hasegawa, Ito, Kawano, Kibata, & Nonomura, 2013). In China, the growth of the game industry has been so rapid that it has emerged to become a global center of game production in less than two decades. In 2016, China surpassed the United States (which had a revenue of US$23.5 billion; Newzoo, 2016) to become the world's largest game market, and it began to export locally developed games worldwide.

An investigation of the development of the game industries and markets in different countries is therefore useful for Hong Kong, in which the public often calls for a cultural policy on certain creative industries. Because of strong national rivalries in East Asia and the huge Asian market (US$46.6 billion), Hong Kong's game industry urgently needs the help of cultural policies, business models, regulation, and industry norms in order to enter the Chinese and East Asian markets. In South Korea, for example, in the past decade, the Korea Game Development and Promotion Institute (KGDPI) and the Korea Culture and Content Agency (KOCCA) constructed extensive and successful policies for developing Korean games. In addition, South Korea's Asian Cultural Policy Network gathers international scholars to discuss the creative industries with Korean officials, industry representatives, and academics. South Korea game companies have also considered developing strategies to fend off global competitors, and in particular, China (Song, 2016).

Even though China did not pay particularly serious attention to the creative industries until the mid-2000s, it is now far ahead of Hong Kong in terms of designing policies for promoting and regulating the game industry. In China, a designated bureau, the Electronic and Internet Publication Section of the General Administration of Press and Publications, is in charge of developing the industry. The State Taxation Administration has introduced new tax laws on virtual game property. Game-relevant legislation has been ratified, and numerous legal cases (e.g. *Li Hongchen v. Beijing North Arctic*) have been fought. In response to a social backlash against highly exploitive games and the online game addiction of students, China has designed anti–game addiction regulations (Golub & Lingley, 2008; Guan, 2008). The state has also set up the National Online Game Publishing Project to encourage the inclusion of local cultural content in games.

The development of the game industries in these Asian countries has a special meaning for the development of the game industry in Hong Kong, particularly with regard to referencing and complementing the perceived competition, market, and model. In addition to its implications for practical economic goals, this book makes an important theoretical contribution to media studies, management studies, globalization studies, and game studies. First, an investigation of the political economy of the game industry in Hong Kong and other countries can shed theoretical light on how the interplay of political factors (e.g., censorship, control, nationalism, and protectionism) and economic factors (e.g., sponsorship, tax, and trade) affect creative industries, particularly their structure, production, distribution, and content as well as the values and lifestyles of those who consume cultural products. Second, this examination of the globalized production and reception of games can enrich our theoretical understanding of cultural globalization and cultural regionalization in East Asia. This book presents the first systematic study to approach games from the angle of the problematics of cultural globalization, including local reception, glocalization strategies, localization of game content, global diffusion of games, and global game cultural asymmetry. Third, this book's focus on seldom-explored cases of game production and consumption (i.e., in Hong Kong and China) will provide an empirical basis for advancing the current debate on a range of major theoretical issues in game studies, including the social impact of games, non-Western game cultures, virtual taxation, virtual property transaction, virtual-world governance, gamer activism, and the formation of game communities.

LOCATING THE TRAJECTORIES OF GAME STUDIES

This study belongs to the academic discipline, or field, of game studies, which encompasses the study of game content, the act of play, the players, the production and consumption processes, and the interaction of all these—that is, gaming culture. It is fair to say that game studies largely originated in the West, and until the past decade no game studies had been conducted in Asia (see Ernkvist & Strom, 2008). Only recently has a systematic history of video games and development in China, Japan, South Korea, and other Asian countries been documented (Wolf, 2015).

However, research on digital games—or gaming in its modern sense—as Frans Mäyrä (2008) suggests, emerged in the 1970s when shooting and action games became the focus of academic studies. These were then followed by studies on role-playing and adventure games in the 1980s and on three-dimensional games in the 1990s. The bulk of massively multiplayer online role-playing games (MMORPG) discussed and examined in this book refer to a new genre of games that emerged along with broadband Internet, which made possible a smooth, massive connection to online gaming activities.

Game or gaming studies have become legitimatized with the emergence of specialized game-related academic journals such as *Simulation and Gaming* (founded in 1970), *Game Studies* (founded in 2001), *Games and Culture* (founded in 2006), *Eludamos* (founded in 2007), *Journal of Gaming and*

Virtual Worlds (founded in 2009), *International Journal of Gaming and Computer-Mediated Simulations* (founded in 2009), and *Games for Health Journal* (founded in 2012). However, under the same umbrella of game studies, the term *gaming studies* can refer to very different areas in different disciplines, from the technical aspects to the sociocultural effects of gaming and the political economy of the game industry. Aside from the technical, design, and engineering aspects and social and cultural domains—although there is consensual agreement on the epistemology of game studies—there are at least two main branches here: the social, psychological effects of gaming, and the critical study of gaming culture, games, and their development.

First, I consider the social psychological effects of gaming by using a social-science approach to gaming, largely relying on lab experiments, surveys, and other quantitative methods of inquiry. My interpretation is that the effects of gaming are an extension of the effects of traditional media. The reason is simple: parents, adults, teachers, and policy makers are as concerned about the effects of the violence in video games as they were about the effects of violence on television. Using a social psychological approach, my focus is on gauging the effects of violent games on behavior, affect and cognition, physiological arousal, and antisocial attitudes and behaviors, particularly in children and adolescents (e.g., Anderson & Bushman, 2001). Bandura's social learning theory is a core theory that is widely applicable to such effects. In general, researchers believe that children can acquire behaviors by observing scenes and imitating the behavior of the characters in audiovisual content, including that of games (Bandura, 1977). The theoretical basis is comprised of the modeling and cognitive processes that underlie game play. The findings of empirical research suggest that the type of violent game has a positive correlation to violent behavior in children and adolescents, but the effect is less than the effect of television violence on aggression (e.g., Sherry, 2001).

My second approach is to examine the cultural effect of gaming. In this approach, games are both a part of and an influence on popular culture because they integrate the use of the Internet, social media, mobile phones, and other digital devices in different locations such as the workplace, home, arcades, museums, and educational institutions. As cultural texts, games can be interpreted as representations of culture according to race (e.g., Sisler, 2008), gender (Fisher & Harvey, 2013), and other social groupings. In cultural studies, games are examined as social practice in everyday life, and thus concepts such as ideology, resistance, hegemony, signification, encoding and decoding, and active reading are applicable when interpreting game consumption and gamer-users (e.g. Taylor, 2006). Adrienne Shaw (2010) further argued that cultural studies on gaming should focus on video games in culture rather than on merely games as culture, which suggests that gaming is a newly constructed culture and that investigators of game culture should re-flect this culture in their critical practice. This argument is in line with Flew and Humphreys (2005), who suggested that games are a new medium that exemplifies a new productive relationship between users and games in social and network settings.

Recently, the discussion of cultural policy has largely penetrated the study of games and culture from the perspective of cultural industries (Fung, 2016). In particular, the involvement of top-down policies inevitably leads to discussions about the politics of intervention, control, and culture, particular-ly when countries such as China attempt to embed dominant ideologies of patriotism in games, censor game content, and use games as soft power in geocultural politics (Jenkins, 2006; Cao & Downing, 2008). Following this line of inquiry, this book identifies the emerging discourse of the rivalry among Hong Kong, China, Japan, and South Korea, and it explicates the ways in which cultural policy plays a vital role in shaping these industries and escalates the competition in the geocultural politics of the East Asian region. Because of the unquestioned rivalry that exists among game indus-tries in the East Asian region, in addition to an analysis of empirical data, I attempt to provide a self-reflexive, critical angle on the neoliberal narrative of game industry development and state-initiated cultural policy. At this point, *neoliberal narrative* refers to the seemingly free market economy, or "invisible hand," of gaming industries, while *cultural policy* denotes a state-implemented, visible policy that interferes with the game market and de-mand.

GAME INDUSTRY STUDIES AS CREATIVE INDUSTRY STUDIES

Clearly there needs to be a specific focus in the present investigation of East Asian rivalry. In this book, I attempt to analyze the content production of the game industry—subsumed under the term *creative industries*—and the con-sumption of games according to existing models of cultural production (Bourdieu, 1993; du Gay, 1997; Griswold, 2003; Peterson & Anand, 2004). Specifically, in this book the entire game industry from production to con-sumption is examined through a mixed approach that includes political econ-omy on one hand and cultural studies on the other hand. With regard to production, the political economy perspective is applicable to an examination of the operation, management, and distribution systems of game industries as well as to the clustering potential of Hong Kong's game industry. From a cultural studies perspective, consumption is considered through investigating gamers' preferences; the political, social, and cultural contexts of game con-sumption; the linkages between game content and production strategies; and the microprocesses of game consumption.

THE POLITICAL ECONOMY OF THE GAME INDUSTRIES

In general, three research paradigms have inspired my application of political economy to the game industries examined in this book: cultural industries, the political economy of communication, and globalization.

Cultural Industries

The study of cultural industries focuses on production and consumption processes, organization and the creative labor market, business strategies, political and economic impact, cultural texts and values, government regulations, urban conditions, and the global context (Hesmondhalgh, 2012; Hartley, 2005; Raffo, O'Connor, Lovatt, & Banks, 2000). Among these aspects, the most relevant to game industries are those that shape or constrain the politics, censorship, and economic environment or, in this case, the creativity of cultural products (Hesmondhalgh, 2012). I suggest that based on the circuit of culture, the study of the game industry as a cultural industry that generates cultural products could shed light on the extent to which the industry copes with political restriction, competition, cultural differences, changing social conditions, and cultural globalization. Many previous studies have adopted similar approaches when examining creative industries other than the game industry, many of which included empirical research conducted in Asia. Michael Keane (2006; 2016) examined how Chinese cultural industries have resisted and accommodated global competition through using special strategies and cultural adaptation. Joseph Chan, Anthony Fung, and Chun Hung Ng (2009) addressed the conditions in which the formulation of a creative cluster could accelerate the development of established cultural industries in Hong Kong.

Political Economy of Communication

In the neo-Marxist legacy of the political economic perspective, studies have examined how capitalist media corporations maximized their economic interests through business behavior, strategies, and structures that eventually shaped the state's regulations and policies regarding those industries (e.g., Murdock, 1982). Other political economic analyses have focused on the process through which the operations of cultural industries evolved into a monopolized media ecology of spatialization, commodification, and globalization (e.g., Mosco, 1996). They also explicated the flexibility of media industry operations in an increasingly globalized context, which helped businesses satisfy political imperatives, local tastes, and market demands (Morley & Robins, 1995; Gershon, 1997; Turner & Jay, 2009). Political economists have argued that media industries directly generate surplus value

through selling entertainment products and indirectly through creating surplus value within other sectors (Garnham, 1990a; 1990b). Games generate
revenue directly as entertainment products, while their secondary trades,
franchised products and accessories, and crossover cultural products with
other media create additional market value. This critical angle contributes to
our current analysis of game industry within a global and capitalist context.

Globalization

Globalization has become the backdrop against which creative industries
operate and develop. Processes of cultural globalization abound in game
products. For example, a medieval fantasy culture has been diffused across
the globe in almost all MMORPG developed in the West. Processes of economic globalization are also observable in coproductions and joint ventures
in the game industries. For example, because of the phenomenal success of
the online games industry in South Korea, global corporations such as Viven-
di have sought partnerships with South Korean companies. The globalization
of the game industry can be seen as a process that simultaneously embodies
globalizing territorization, local involvement and accommodation, cross-cultural challenges, and dynamics (Giddens, 1991). In this process are alternate
processes of globalization, localization, and glocalization that engender local
resistance (Wilson & Dissanayake, 1996); the coexistence of global and local
forms (Dirlik, 1996); and the hybridization of mixed and creolized cultures
(Pieterse, 1995).

Understanding the political economy of the game industry in general is
not a mere theoretical exercise. Indeed, political and social constraints can
generate obstacles as well as opportunities for this industry. For example,
political censorship of media content poses a problem for Asian game industries that target the Chinese market, and Hong Kong's entertainment industries have been searching for ways to circumvent this problem. An examination of Hong Kong's game industry must include ways to circumvent censorship by Chinese authorities and at the same time gain financial benefit from
this. At the same time, because it is located in the East Asian market, Hong
Kong's game industry also enjoys an advantageous position with regard to
Chinese gamers in the region via cultural proximity and the potential for
cross-border coproduction.

CREATIVE CLUSTERING OF THE GAME INDUSTRY
WITH RELEVANT INDUSTRIES

Any study of the game industry inevitably extends to a subarea of creative
industries, or "creative clustering," particularly in Asia. In Asia, conscious
efforts are being made to build infrastructure, pull together creative indus-

tries, and attract investment by the government in specially designated regions and in technology and science parks in which creative industries are expected to perform more effectively and efficiently with governmental support. In general, government officials and some scholars agree that such creative clusters are crucial in developing creative industries and a cultural economy (Florida, 2003; Cooke & Lazzeretti, 2008; Kong, 2009). However, other scholars have been more cautious. The seamless logistics assumed by such promoters of a cultural economy driven by infrastructure, software, and labor could, these scholars say, lead to system breakdown (Rossiter, 2016), and an uncritical indulgence in gentrification and the new cultural economy could lead to a new generation of neobohemians (Lloyd, 2010). Furthermore, because of increasingly unequal and precarious work conditions, scholars such as Mark Banks (2017) have called for creative justice.

In reality, such ideals and normative discussions are not given much credence. International nongovernmental organizations (NGOs) such as UNESCO as well as cities and local regions in the developed world and in Asia, including Hong Kong, eagerly seek practical ways to build creative clusters and cultural economy (Bauhinia Foundation Research Centre, 2007; New England Council, 2001; UNESCO, 2009). The video game industries form an ecosystem that is highly dependent on structures and interactions within itself (Zackariasson, 2014). For example, China has been aggressive in its attempt to construct creative clusters (Keane, 2009). As a regional center of pop culture production in the past few decades, Hong Kong is already a powerful creative cluster that consists of the pop music, film, fashion, entertainment, and advertising industries. Currently however, Hong Kong's game industry is neither well integrated into this cluster nor has it capitalized on the cluster's resources. Although studies conducted in the West have begun to pay attention to the potential synergy between games and other pop culture genres, no proven business models or cases have emerged that illustrate the economic multiplier effect of such a synergy.

Nevertheless, it is likely that the multiplier effect would be positive and that the Hong Kong, Chinese, and East Asian markets would be receptive to this synergy. Hollywood gaming is a global pioneer in devising synergetic ventures because of its experience in synergizing with other entertaining industries (e.g., videos, games, and films; Brookey, 2010). The process of synergy and clustering faces numerous technical and social network obstacles, however. For example, although the integration of pop-up or product placement advertisements in game content is common, creative workers and management in the game industry are not well networked with those in the pop music, film, fashion, and entertainment industries. Moreover, few studies have examined the effect of labor conditions in the West and in Asia (e.g., Curtin & Sanson, 2016).

In addition to the pop culture industries, the game industry constitutes a cultural industry with a large economic multiplier effect. Besides the direct revenue generated by games, the game industry also drives virtual property transactions and other cultural productions along the value chain of the game industry. The total wealth generated by this industry has been estimated to be close to that of the online game industry itself (Castronova, 2004). The global turnover of virtual property transactions grew from a negligible amount in the late 1990s to US$2.09 billion in 2006 (Lehtiniemi & Lehdon-virta, 2007), and it was particularly strong in Asia. Virtual property transactions on mobile devices in China achieved a record high of US$6 trillion in the first quarter of 2016 (iResearch, 2016), and the regulation, ethics, and control of virtual economy and property have become a debatable issue in China (Chew, 2015). Furthermore, as mobile games become increasingly popular (in addition to online games), the virtual property industry will grow even more rapidly. Because this industry is informal and underground, few scholars, policy makers, or business leaders have proposed ways for Hong Kong to develop it. However, Hong Kong is nonetheless in a unique position to benefit from this industry. Around 80 percent of all virtual property production in the world is currently carried out in China (Heeks, 2008). IGE, a previously dominant global corporation of virtual property transactions, international gaming, and entertainment had to base its operations in Hong Kong, for example. Business strategies and long-term cultural policies that tap into the economy of the virtual property industry are also a potential area of research.

CREATIVE LABOR OF THE GAME INDUSTRIES

Research has been conducted on the work and the workers of the creative industries (Sussman & Lent, 1998; Beck, 2002; Florida, 2003), but few studies have focused on those of the game industries. Although the game industry has expanded successfully in the past decade in many countries, the substantial profits accrued were not necessarily reinvested in the education and rewarding of creative talent in the industry. The exploitation of creative labor is certainly not limited to the game industry (Rodino-Colocino, 2006). However, with the exception of software, because very few creative products are as authorless as game products are, creative labor in the game industry is more susceptible to undervaluation than in other creative industries. This problem is not yet significant in Hong Kong because the largest game companies are only medium size, but it is likely to surface as the game industry develops in Hong Kong and in other Asian countries.

CONSUMERS AND THE CONSUMPTION OF GAMES

The concept of *active audiences* has emerged in the field of cultural studies. In the age of digitalization, scholars such as John Hartley (2005) define as "active" those consumers who could be seen as creative labor and who could be conceptualized as a major and indispensable productive force. Consumers of creative products can affect the productive process and creative work in numerous ways in addition to their purchase choices. Recent research in cultural studies, media studies, and business studies have highlighted the proactive and participatory roles of consumers in coproducing cultural products with creative workers (Jenkins, Ito, & Boyd, 2015). Research in cultural economics and the creative industry has identified social network effects among consumers' and conceptualized consumers' tastes and word-of-mouth as information feedback about creative work in the industries (Potts, Cunningham, Hartley, & Ormerod, 2008; Potts, Hartley, Banks, & Burgess, 2008; Uricchio, 2004).

Among all creative industries, the game industry is the most advanced in terms of incorporating consumers' free labor in the cocreation of game products (Humphreys, 2005a, 2005b; Banks & Potts, 2010). Online game companies rely on gamers to maintain sociality and order within virtual worlds as well as to generate new game features. They depend on gamers' free labor in programming game mods, testing play, and giving detailed feedback. Most importantly, game companies have already incorporated these consumers' contributions in their business models and in design arrangements that facilitate cocreation.

In the communication process, conventional approaches to gamers as media audience are also applicable to the study of gamers. For example, the differences between the online and offline lives of gamers and their values, identities, and community formations are common research topics in game studies (Fung, 2009). Previous research has concluded with the fact that gamers in the cyber world are active audience that engages in playful acts of subversion and appropriation to resist game companies and the government, especially in the Chinese context (Behrenshausen, 2013). The social implications of game consumption should also be considered when we are devising cultural policies that both minimize negative effects and satisfy market forces.

THE SCOPE AND CONTENT OF THIS BOOK

This book is both a critical academic study and a policy study of Hong Kong's game industry in the context of Asian competition against the backdrop of a global gaming culture. First, my academic and intellectual lines of inquiry are based on approaches used in political economic and cultural studies. Second, in addition to these academic analyses, this is a study of policies that could animate and enhance the cultural practices, agency, and subjectivity of the players involved. With this novel approach, I attempt to determine implications for policy by considering how the empirical data collected in this theory-informed study could serve the development of the game industry in Hong Kong (a commercial goal), enable the entire cultural economy of Hong Kong (a cultural and commercial goal), and celebrate the city's social values (a social goal).

I would like to emphasize that the last goal—in pursuit of a higher social goal—is unique in this critical approach to cultural policy. Although there is no single definition of what is "critical" in this study on cultural policy, we can understand that it inherits the progressive energies and radical dynamics of political economy and cultural studies. It does not aim to serve the state but to draw attention to important global values such as global citizenship, freedom, and cultural rights (Lewis & Miller, 2002). Furthermore, in this critical approach to the study of the game industry, recommendations for cultural policy are not the goal. Instead, any recommendations are only one means by which the Hong Kong public might sustain its values, creativity, freedom, and ideals.

The scope of this book extends to the game industries in the East Asian countries of Hong Kong, China, South Korea, and Japan. Specifically, "East Asian" here mainly refers to Hong Kong, China, South Korea, and Japan. Singapore is not included in this study simply because little original game production takes place there, although some publishers in Singapore market online games. In Taiwan, although there is active production of original online games, in the East Asian discourse this country is not acknowledged as a power center. I have also not included Taiwan in order to avoid exacerbating the debate over the unification of China and Taiwan and the cultural politics related to this. Furthermore, I emphasize that there is no simple way to understand East Asia, but there are specific political, economic, social, and cultural contexts in which the creative industries in East Asia operate (Lee & Lim, 2014). Accordingly, I use various kinds of data to provide detailed descriptions, analyses, and comparisons of the game industries and cultural policies in this region. Based on these data, I analyze and explicate the discourse of East Asian rivalry, and then I attempt to determine the implications this has for Hong Kong's creative and game industries—which is the ultimate goal of this book.

The East Asian (most notably South Korea and Japan) and American markets have shown that gaming, its secondary markets, and its creative clustering with other creative industries can be an important contributor to GDP. Therefore, this book presents a baseline study that is pertinent to Hong Kong's game industry, its potential market, and its social effects. The results provide information for a coherent cultural policy for developing this emerging creative industry and exploiting its synergy with other creative industries, talents, and products.

It is true that scholars in the field have focused on Internet culture, the online world, social media, and emerging media. However, few of these studies include games, which are still marginalized in academic discourse. Nevertheless, games are well integrated into the daily lives of citizens as a mainstream form of digital entertainment, a site of education, and even as a profession. Games are more ubiquitous than many media and platforms are. This book responds to this cultural phenomenon by gauging the social and cultural effects generated by gaming, especially in Hong Kong, where reports have hinted at the negative psychological effects of games (including addiction), their pornographic and violent content, and the social conflict they have triggered via online disputes through mass media.

Because of a perceived urgent need for relevant information and policies, this book provides a comprehensive study of the game industry in Hong Kong from an international, comparative perspective. Based on empirical data collected in Hong Kong, China, Asia, and other areas, the study presented in this book analyzes major cultural policies in the East Asian region that are potential blueprints that may allow the Hong Kong government to develop the game industry and regulate the social effects of gaming. Based on data collected from consumers of games and cases of successful game industries, the results could be used to devise business strategies for Hong Kong's game industry to expand its operations and markets in China and East Asia. The significance of these strategies lies not only in boosting Hong Kong's economy and exports but also in constructing an image of Hong Kong as a regional hub of creative industries in Asia. The policy implications of this project are significant not merely for the game industry but also for Hong Kong's existing creative clusters (film, pop music, television, design, fashion, and advertising), which confront Asian competitors that aggressively cultivate their own creative industries (i.e., those in South Korea, Japan, and China). With regard to the theoretical implications of this study, my investigation of the political economy of game industries, creative labor, and consumption will enhance our understanding of the issues and challenges of games on a micro level as well as the role of games in the emerging cultural economy of global cities on a macro level.

My study follows games from their production and distribution to their consumption in specific Asian contexts. The structure of game industries, their sociopolitical contexts, cultural policies, corporations, and production and distribution are analyzed from the perspective of political economy. A cultural studies perspective is employed to interpret the interaction of players and gamers. Although the setting of the study is Hong Kong because it is inevitably drawn into the vortex of Asian rivalry and the Chinese market, the Chinese and Asian markets and various Asian game models are considered.

First, the book examines the major issues and challenges in Hong Kong's game industry, including its potential social effects. It then proposes possible regulations, cultural policies, and strategies for development. Because of an ever-increasing crossover between the game industry and other local, related creative industries (i.e., the music, film, and new media industries), the book also suggests strategies for the development of the entire creative industry in Hong Kong. Second, given the increasing prominence of the game industry and its success in many Asian countries, this book examines opportunities for the Hong Kong game industry, particularly in the China and Asian markets.

I attempt to present empirical data collected firsthand in the past few years in addition to background and secondary data. In the following chapters, I will refer to various findings and evidence to substantiate my argument that Hong Kong's game industry is a creative industry and to support my views on perceived Asian rivalries.

RESEARCH METHODS AND DESIGN

The study presented in this book is based on data collected by multiple interdisciplinary methods from 2011 to 2015, which were supplemented by updated documents and follow-up interviews conducted in 2016 and 2017 during my involvement in the industry study "Digital Entertainment Survey" by CreateHK. The methods employed include organizational analyses (political economy), textual analysis of game content (media studies), questionnaire surveys of gamers (sociology), participant observation (anthropology), and policy analyses.

The Interview Process

To understand the operation and structure of Hong Kong game companies and their challenges and opportunities, I interviewed key figures in Hong Kong's game industry. In addition to open information and documented data, interviewing is considered a core method for institutional analysis. Also interviewed were owners and managers in the game industry (including the owner of the first publicly listed Hong Kong company, Gameone Group); organizers of professional bodies in the game industry (e.g., the Hong Kong Game Industry Association and the Hong Kong Game Development Association); creative workers (e.g., game artists, designers, and programmers); and the marketers and distributors of game companies. The owners and managers of cyber cafes and game arcades were also interviewed. In Hong Kong, more than forty of these key individuals were interviewed multiple times (some of the interviews were informal). Most interviewees were referred by the Hong

Kong Game Industry Association (HKGIA). At the beginning of this process, I was invited to various public functions organized by the industry. In particular, based on the findings of my study, I gave a speech on behalf of Hong Kong's game industry at the Asian Online Game Award ceremony in 2011. In 2012, I was appointed a consultant of HKGIA, and I now attend regular meetings of the association. In 2016, I became an independent, non-executive director of Gameone Group when it was listed on the Hong Kong Stock Exchange. In early 2016, I was in charge of an industry survey of digital entertainment sponsored by CreateHK, the governmental department responsible for creative industries. Different industry associations, including HKGIA, aim at gauging the scale of the industry, its challenges, and its opportunities (Hong Kong Digital Entertainment Association, 2017).

During the study period, as I interviewed different stakeholders and held regular meetings with them, I felt that I was becoming a member of the Hong Kong game industry. All these activities went beyond what a typical researcher might do. Thus, in writing this book, while I intended to write in-depth about the gaming industry in Hong Kong, I was also self-reflexive in the process. Since becoming an independent, non-executive director of Gameone Group in 2016, I have been involved in real industry practices and businesses, and I have met many professionals in the game industry and other related industries.

I also interviewed members of game companies in other countries. In China, in collaboration with the Institute of Cultural Industries at Peking University, my research assistants and I interviewed more than sixty individuals, including officials and policy makers who were responsible for implementing and regulating censorship, cultural policies, and the legal framework of the game industry. Some interviews were conducted with individuals, and others were conducted in the form of focus groups.

With regard to the East Asian countries of Korea and Japan, I traveled to Seoul to interview professionals, gamers, and government officials. In Japan, I interviewed scholars, gamers, cultural critics, and other individuals in the creative industries. To gain a broad picture of the creative industries and the game industries in these countries, my research team and I also made observations in active game production hubs and conducted interviews of game importers in Asia, including Singapore, Malaysia, Thailand, and Vietnam, which are major sites for the consumption of games. An international team of researchers conducted original empirical research in these countries. Based on these empirical studies and secondary data, my research team wrote reports on China, Japan, South Korea, Southeast Asia, Europe, North America, and Australia. In some chapters of this book, I will draw upon the findings in these research reports and data collected in the interviews, which are publicly available on the project's website http://creativeindustries.com.cuhk.edu.hk.

Because of the complex interview conditions in the different countries, it is impossible to provide the actual interview questions. In addition to collecting data about the game industry, consumption, and the market, the interviews were all aimed at solving the predicament of Hong Kong's game industry in the context of keen Asian competition and a huge China market. The study is based on a grounded analysis method, and multiple interviews were sometimes conducted to refine concepts and thoughts.

The Study of Gamers as Audience

The primary focus of this book is the game industry. My study method combines approaches used in political economy and cultural studies. On one hand, my political-economic analysis of institutions is mainly based on interviews with personnel in the game industry. More than sixty interviews conducted in China, more than twenty interviews in Hong Kong, and more than thirty interviews in the other countries and regions (South Korea, Japan, Vietnam, Thailand, and Malaysia). Also, from the perspective of cultural studies, in addition to critical analyses of cultural policy, game use, and gaming, my understanding of the audience of gamers was supplemented by data collected in a systematic survey and from thirty in-depth interviews with players in Hong Kong and China.

The survey, which was designed to generate an overall picture of game consumption, targeted game-playing individuals between fourteen and forty-five years old. This age range of the gamers deserves an explanation. Because games are a mainstream form of entertainment that is consumed by people in different age groups (e.g., in the United States, the average age of the online gamer is twenty-eight), my survey did not focus exclusively on youths and adolescents. Thus a wider age range was adopted for this study. In 2011, a telephone survey was implemented to collect eight hundred representative samples to probe respondents' consumption practices, values, psychographics, socioeconomic attributes, and reception of clustered products in Hong Kong. To understand the players, I also went to different public game events, including Animation-Comic-Game Hong Kong (ACGHK), an annual game fair, to talk to the gamers in attendance.

In addition to the information collected by interviews and surveys, participant observations (i.e., online participant observations) were made at major game sites in Hong Kong and China, including cyber cafes, arcades, and game virtual worlds, which provided data on the popularity of games, games consumed, and the gaming context. In 2011, with the collaboration of the Hong Kong Internet Café Association, a systematic survey with face-to-face questionnaire interviews was conducted in Internet cafes in different districts of Hong Kong using stratified sampling.

A Comparative Perspective

The fieldwork was conducted mainly in Hong Kong because the focus of this book is the game industry in Hong Kong. I want to emphasize the book's comparative approach to cultural policies, regulations, creative clustering, industrial development strategies, consumption practices, and game markets in China, South Korea, and Japan. The growth, development, and prospects of Hong Kong's game industry are always discussed in comparison to or in relation to other countries. In particular, the Hong Kong game market, as compared to the East Asian market, is a consistent theme throughout the book.

REFERENCES

Anderson, C., and Bushman, B. (2001). Effects of violent video games on aggressive behavior, aggressive cognition, aggressive affect, physiological arousal, and prosocial behavior: A meta-analytic review of the scientific literature. *Psychological Science, 12*(5), 353–359.

ANI-com. (2015). The 17th HKACG 2015. Retrieved from http://www.ani-com.hk/2015ver/pdf/2015%20ACGHK_Info_Chi.pdf .

Bandura, A. (1977). *Social learning theory*. New York: General Learning Press.

Banks, J., and Potts, J. (2010). Co-creating games: A co-evolutionary analysis. *New Media & Society, 12*(2), 253–270.

Banks, M. (2017). *Creative justice: Cultural industries, work and inequality*. Lanham, MD: Rowman & Littlefield.

Bauhinia Foundation Research Centre. (2007). Hong Kong: A creative metropolis. A policy submission paper. Retrieved from http://www.ccif.hk/index.php/en/links.

Beck, U. (2002). The cosmopolitan society and its enemies. *Theory, Culture & Society, 19*(1–2), 17–44.

Behrenshausen, B. (2013) The active audience, again: Player-centric game studies and the problem of binarism. *New Media & Society, 15*(6): 872–889.

Beijing News. (2017). 13-year-old youth plays King of Glory. After waking up, why couldn't I fly? [13岁少年玩王者荣耀跳楼 醒后称：我怎么不会飞]. *Sina News*. Retrieved from http://news.sina.com.cn/s/qw/2017-07-03/doc-ifyhrxsk1585776.shtml.

Bourdieu, P. (1993). *Field of cultural production*. New York: Columbia University Press.

Brookey, R. A. (2010). *Hollywood gamers: Digital convergence in the film and video game industries*. Bloomington, IN: Indiana University Press.

Cao, Y., and Downing, J. (2008). The realities of virtual play: Video games and their industry in China. *Journal of Media, Culture & Society, 30*(4), 515–529.

Castronova, E. (2004). The right to play. *NY Law School Review, 49*(1), 185–210.

Central Policy Unit. (2003). Baseline study of Hong Kong's creative industries. Retrieved from http://www.cpu.gov.hk/doc/en/research_reports/baseline%20study(eng).pdf.

Chan, D. (2012). Beyond the "Great Firewall": The case of in-game protests in China. In L. Hjorth and D. Chan (Eds.), *Gaming cultures and place in the Asia-Pacific* (pp. 141–157). London: Routledge.

Chan, J., Fung, A., and Ng, C. H. (2009). *Policies for a sustainable development of the Hong Kong film industry*. Hong Kong: Hong Kong Institute for Asia-Pacific Studies.

Chew, M. (2015). Online game and society in China: An exploration of key issues and challenges. In L. Hjorth and O. Khoo (Eds.), *Routledge handbook of new media in Asia* (pp. 391–401). London: Routledge.

Cooke, P. N., and Lazzeretti, L. (Eds.). (2008). *Creative cities, cultural clusters and local economic development*. Cheltenham, UK: Edward Elgar Publishing.

Curtin, M., and Sanson, M. (2016). *Precarious creativity: Global media, local labor.* Berkeley: University of California Press.
DFC. (2016, April). Research brief: Video game market overview. Retrieved from http://www.dfcint.com/wp/product/video-game-market-overview/.
Dirlik, A. (1996). The global in the local. In R. Wilson and W. Dissanayake (Eds.), *Global/local: Cultural production and the transnational imaginary* (pp. 21–45). Durham, NC: Duke University Press.
Du Gay, P. (Ed.). (1997). *Production of culture/ cultures of production.* London: Sage Publications.
Ernkvist, M., and Strom, P. (2008). Enmeshed in games with the government: Governmental policies and the development of the Chinese online game industry. *Games and Culture, 3*(1), 98–126.
Fisher, S., and Harvey, A. (2013). Intervention for inclusivity: Gender politics and indie game development. *Loading, 7*(11), 25–40.
Fiske, J. (1989). *Reading the popular.* New York: Routledge.
Flew, T., and Humphreys, S. (2005). Games: Technology, industry, culture (2nd ed.) In T. Flew (Ed.), *New media: An introduction* (pp. 101–114). Oxford: Oxford University Press.
Florida, R. (2003). Cities and the creative class. *City and Community, 2*, 3–19.
Fung, A. (2006). Bridging cyberlife and real life: A study of online communities in Hong Kong. In D. Silver, A. Massanari, and S. Jones (Eds.), *Critical cyberculture reader* (pp. 129–139). New York: New York University Press.
Fung, A. (2008). *Global capital, local culture: Transnational media corporations in China.* New York: Peter Lang.
Fung, A. (2009). Online games, cyberculture and community: The deterritorization and crystallization of community space. In L. Leung, A. Fung, and P. Lee (Eds.), *Embedding into our lives: New opportunities and challenges of the internet* (pp. 189–205). Hong Kong: Chinese University Press.
Fung, A. (Ed). (2016). *Global game industries and culture policy.* London: Palgrave Macmillan.
Garnham, N. (1990a). *Capitalism and communication: Global culture and the economics of information* (Media Culture & Society series). Newbury Park, CA: Sage Publications.
Garnham, N. (1990b). Public policy and the cultural industries. In F. Inglis (Ed.), *Capitalism and communication: Global culture and the economics of information* (pp.155–168). London: Sage Publications.
Gershon, R. (1997). *The transnational media corporation: Global messages and free market competition.* Mahwah, NJ: Lawrence Erlbaum Associates.
Giddens, A. (2003). *Runaway world: How globalization is shaping our lives.* New York: Routledge.
Golub, A., and Lingley, K. (2008). "Just like the Qing empire": Internet addiction, MMOGs, and moral crisis in contemporary China. *Games and Culture, 3*(1), 59–75.
Griswold, W. (2003). *Cultures and societies in a changing world* (2nd ed.). Thousand Oaks, CA: Sage Publications.
Guan, I. (2008). *Information inequality and Chinese online game: A case study of ZT online* (Unpublished Master's thesis). Chinese University of Hong Kong.
Hartley, J. (2005). *Creative industries.* Malden, MA: Blackwell.
Hasegawa, T., Ito, T., Kawano, R., Kibata, K., and Nonomura, K. (2013). The Japanese gaming cluster. Unpublished manuscript. Retrieved from http://www.isc.hbs.edu/resources/courses/moc-course-at-harvard/Documents/pdf/student-projects/Final%20paper%20-%20Japan%20gaming%20cluster%20vfinal.pdf.
Heeks, R. (2008). Current analysis and future research agenda on "gold-farming." Working paper. *Development Informatics, 32.*
Hesmondhalgh, D. (2012). *The cultural industries* (3rd ed.). Thousand Oaks, CA: Sage Publications.
Hong Kong Digital Entertainment Association. (2017) Survey on "Hong Kong digital entertainment industry:" executive report. Hong Kong: Centre for Communication and Public Opinion Survey, Chinese University of Hong Kong.

Humphreys, S. (2005a). Productive players: Online computer games' challenge to conventional media forms. *Communication and Critical/Cultural Studies, 2*(1), 37–51.

Humphreys, S. (2005b). Productive users, intellectual property and governance: The challenges of computer games. *Media and Arts Law Review, 10*(4), 299–310.

iResearch. (2016). China's third-party mobile payment GMV broke 6 Tn Yuan in Q1 2016. Retrieved from http://www.iresearchchina.com/content/details7_24301.html.

Jenkins, H. (2006). National politics within virtual game worlds: The case of China. Retrieved from http://www.henryjenkins.org/2006/08/national_politics_within_virtu_1.html.

Jenkins, H., Ito, M., and Boyd, D. (2015). *Participatory culture in a networked era: A conversation on youth, learning, commerce and politics.* London: Polity.

Jin, D. Y. (2010). *Korea's online gaming empire.* Cambridge, MA: MIT Press.

Keane, M. (2006). Once were peripheral: Creating media capacity in East Asia. *Media, Culture and Society, 28*(6), 835–855.

Keane, M. (2009). Great adaptations: China's creative clusters and the new social contract. *Continuum: Journal of Media & Cultural Studies, 23*(2), 221–230.

Keane, M. (2016). *Handbook of cultural and creative industries in China.* Cheltenham, UK: Edward Elgar Publishing.

Kong, L. (2009). Making sustainable creative/cultural space in Shanghai and Singapore. *Geographical Review, 99*(1), 1–22.

KPMG. (2007). Video games market in China: Moving online. Retrieved from http://trpc.biz/wp-content/uploads/2008-07_KPMG_VideoGamesInChinaMovingOnline_Report.pdf.

Kshetri, N. (2010). The evolution of the Chinese online gaming industry. *Journal of Technology Management in China, 4*(2), 158–179.

Lee, H., and Lim, H. (2014). *Cultural Policies in East Asia: Dynamics between the state, arts and creative industries.* London: Palgrave Macmillan.

Lehtiniemi, T., and Lehdonvirta, V. (2007). How big is the RMT market anyway? [Retrieved from https://virtualeconomyresearchnetwork.wordpress.com/2007/03/02/how_big_is_the_rmt_market_anyw/.

Lewis, J., and Miller, T. (2002). *Critical cultural policy: A reader.* Malden, MA: Wiley-Blackwell.

Lloyd, R. (2010). *Neo-bohemia art and commerce in the postindustrial city* (2nd ed.). London: Routledge.

Lossiter, N. (2016). *Software, infrastructure, labor: A media theory of logistical nightmares.* London: Routledge.

Mäyrä, F. (2008). *An introduction to game studies: Games and culture.* London: Sage Publications.

Morley, D., and Robins, D. (1995). *Spaces of identity: Global media, electronic landscapes and cultural boundaries.* New York: Routledge.

Mosco, V. (1996). *The political economy of communication: Rethinking and renewal.* Thousand Oaks, CA: Sage Publications.

Murdock, G. (1982). Large corporations and the control of communications industries. In M. Gurevitch, J. Curran, and J. Woollacott (Eds.), *Culture, society and the media* (pp. 118–150). New York: Methuen.

New England Council. (2001). The creative economy initiative: A blueprint for investment in New England's creative economy. https://www.nefa.org/about-us/publications.

Newzoo. (2016). The global games market reaches $99.6 billon in 2016, mobile generating 33.7 percent. Retrieved from https://newzoo.com/insights/articles/global-games-market-reaches-99-6-billion-2016-mobile-generating-37/.

People.cn. (2017). People.cn criticized King of Glory: Is it entertaining the public or "jeopardizing" life? [人民网一评《王者荣耀》：是娱乐大众还是"陷害"人生] Retrieved from http://opinion.people.com.cn/n1/2017/0703/c1003-29379751.html.

Peterson, R. A., and Anand, N. (2004). The production of culture perspective. *Annual Review of Sociology, 30*, 311–334.

Pieterse J. N. (1995). "Globalization as Hybridization." http://www.uvm.edu/rsenr/rm230/Nederveen%20Pieterse.pdf.

Potts, J., Cunningham, S., Hartley, J., and Ormerod, P. (2008). Social network markets: A new definition of the creative industries. *Journal of Cultural Economics, 32*(3), 167–185.

Potts, J., Hartley, J., Banks, J., Burgess, J., Cobcroft, R., Cunningham, S., and Montgomery, L. (2008). Consumer co-creation and situated creativity. *Industry and Innovation 15*(5), 459–474.

Raffo, C., O'Connor, J., Lovatt, A., and Banks, M. (2000). Teaching and learning entrepreneurship for micro and small businesses in the cultural industries sector. *Education and Training, 46*(6), 356–365.

Rodino-Colocino, M. (2006). Laboring under the digital divide. *New Media & Society, 8*(3), 487–511.

Rossiter, N. (2016). *Software, infrastructure, labor: A media theory of logistical nightmares.* London: Routledge.

Shaw, A. (2010). What is video game culture? Cultural studies and game studies. *Games and Culture, 5*(4), 403–424.

Sherry, J. (2001). The effect of violent video games on aggression: A meta-analysis. *Human Communication Research, 27*(3), 409–431.

Sisler, V. (2008). Digital Arabs: Representation in video games. *European Journal of Cultural Studies, 11*(2), 203–220.

Song, J. (2016). South Korea gaming groups struggle to fend off China. *Financial Times.* Retrieved from https://www.ft.com/content/c1696490-69f7-11e6-a0b1-d87a9fea034f.

Statista. (2016a). Game market revenue in South Korea from 2013 to 2017. Retrieved from http://www.statista.com/statistics/248666/game-sales-in-south-korea/.

Statista. (2016b). Game market revenue in Japan from 2008 to 2017. Retrieved from http://www.statista.com/statistics/260176/video-game-revenue-in-japan.

Sussman, G., and Lent, J. (1998). *Global productions: Labor in the making of the information society.* Cresskill, NJ: Hampton Press.

Taylor, T. L. (2006). *Play between worlds: Exploring online game culture.* Cambridge, MA: MIT Press.

Turner, G., and Jay, T. (Eds.). (2009). *Television studies after TV.* London: Routledge.

UNESCO (2009). The 2009 UNESCO framework for cultural statistics (FCS). Retrieved from http://unesdoc.unesco.org/images/0019/001910/191061e.pdf.

Uricchio, W. (2004). Beyond the great divide: Collaborative networks and the challenge to dominant conceptions of creative industries. *International Journal of Cultural Studies, 7*(1), 79–90.

Wilson, R., and Dissanayake, W. (1996). Introduction: Tracking the global/local. In *Global/local: Cultural production and the transnational imaginary* (pp. 1–18). Durham, NC: Duke University Press.

Wolf, M. (Ed.). (2015). *Video games around the world.* Boston. MA: MIT Press.

Zackariasson, P. (Ed). (2014). *The video game industry.* London: Routledge.

Zhang, H. [張賀]. (2017). Why do mobile phones become "digital opium"? [手机为何成了"电子鸦片"]. *People's Daily.* Retrieved from http://paper.people.com.cn/rmrb/html/2017-07/13/nw.D110000renmrb_20170713_2-19.htm.

Chapter Two

Development and Market Structure of the Creative Industries in Hong Kong

According to official public discourse, which used to emphasize only the financial and tourism industries, the creative industries are now important economic drivers in Hong Kong. To a certain extent, they benefit Hong Kong by adding extra revenue to the economy and by providing job opportunities. Although the total market size of the creative industries continues to expand, the development of different sectors in the industry has varied. This chapter will introduce the creative industries in Hong Kong and then analyze the development and market structure of the creative industries—particularly that of the game industry since 2005.

INTRODUCTION TO HONG KONG'S CREATIVE INDUSTRIES

The Hong Kong Special Administrative Region (HKSAR) has publicly acknowledged its adoption of the term *creative industries*, which was used by Hong Kong's colonizer, the United Kingdom. In the UK government's "Creative Industries Mapping Document," creative industries are defined as "those industries which have their origin in individual creativity, skill and talent and which have a potential for wealth and job creation through the generation and exploitation of intellectual property" (UK Department of Culture, Media and Sport, 1998). In economic transformation, developed countries gradually move their heavy industries to developing countries, which results in a new form of domestic industry that largely deals with the innova-

23

tion, production, and distribution of products and services, which ultimately leads to creativity. This trend and the discourse of creative industries is prevalent in an increasing number of countries such as the United States, South Korea, Japan, Germany, France, Italy, Australia, New Zealand, and China, which have declared a deep interest in developing their own cultural industries. Hong Kong is surrounded by the strong nations of Japan, South Korea, and China, which "threaten" its economic power as a growing international and cosmopolitan global city. Consequently, Hong Kong cannot lag behind the current drive to develop and market creative industries. In addition, Hong Kong rarely admits that it learns from the creative industries of other countries, particularly those of the other Asian "dragons," South Korea, Taiwan, and Singapore.

According to the University of Hong Kong Centre for Cultural Policy Research (2003), the term *creative industries* refers to "a group of economic activities that exploit and deploy creativity, skill and intellectual property to produce and distribute products and services of social and cultural meaning" (p. 22). These economic activities are expected to generate wealth and jobs, which I argue fall into the dominant discourse of the HKSAR: creative industries are a cultural means of making a profit in this capitalist society.

Based on the international statistical guidelines of the United Nations and the local economic situation in Hong Kong, the local creative industries are classified in this study into eleven sectors: art, antiques and crafts; cultural education and libraries; archive and museum services; performing arts; film, video and music; television and radio; publishing; software, computer games, and interactive media (SCGIM); design and architecture; advertising; and amusement services. Recently, based on this classification, Hong Kong claimed that it had developed a lead in the key sectors of these creative industries. Official statistics showed that its creative industries added a value to Hong Kong's GDP of over HKD$90 billion annually and contributed to 4.9 percent of total GDP (Hong Kong Census and Statistics Department, 2014a).

THE MARKET STRUCTURE OF
HONG KONG'S CREATIVE INDUSTRIES

The HKSAR emphasizes the development of local creative industries based on free competition. This noninterventionist strategy is based on the logic that free competition will lower entry barriers to both sellers and buyers. According to the Hong Kong Information Services Department (2013), around 36,000 establishments were related to the creative industries, and more than 192,000 practitioners worked in these industries, which the government viewed as evidence of the vibrancy of the creative industries in

Hong Kong. However, to what degree do these statistics reflect a true picture?

The aim of this book is provide a critical evaluation of these figures in the context of Hong Kong. At the end of 2013, the population in Hong Kong was about 7.2 million, which included a large workforce (Hong Kong Census and Statistics Department, 2014b). However, how many workers were employed in the creative industries? Moreover, the official statistics published by the Annual Survey of Economic Activities (ASEA) listed the "value added" of the eleven sectors that were claimed to be domains of the creative industries in Hong Kong (see figure 2.1; Hong Kong Census and Statistics Department, 2014a). Based on these data, the authorities then proceeded to extrapolate the entire market of the creative industries and their sectors (Hong Kong Census and Statistics Department, 2014a). However, from the point of view of a critical inquiry, is such an extrapolation accurate?

It should be noted that many of the areas classified as creative industries in this report would not fall into the category of creative industries that are examined in this present book and would not be regarded as such in our definition. The sector of art, antiques, and crafts refers mainly to the manufacture and retailing of jewelry and related articles. In 2012, the value added of this industry was HKD$11.45 billion. The retail jewelry sector in Hong Kong has expanded in recent years partly because of high demand from mainland China visitors. Consequently, this growing sector provided more job opportunities for the workforce. Nevertheless, neither the GDP nor the new positions created correctly reflect the creative production of the city. Research in countries that are dependent on their creative industries (e.g., Kakiuchi & Takeuchi, 2014) has indicated that official classification of creative industries leads to a misleading picture. The evidence suggests that many culturally led industries are becoming increasingly noncreative.

The same statistical report, not surprisingly, includes culturally led industries that may not in fact be productively creative. Some of these sectors are marginal, such as the sectors of cultural education, libraries, archives, museum services, and historical sites (which is an important indicator of Hong Kong's cultural policy). The performing arts, the smallest of Hong Kong's creative industries, include creative and performing art activities as well as the agents of artists and models. Although such arts-related sectors could be said to be part of the creative industries, they differ from the game, comics, and animation sector, the operation of which involves mass production and distribution.

The mass media are at the core of the creative industries. Before 2000, in the so-called golden years of Hong Kong's film and popular music industries, Cantopop was predominant. In 2012, the production and distribution of films, videos, and music had an added value of HKD$3.64 billion in the local creative industries. In 2012, the television and radio industry, which included all electronic broadcasting activities via land, satellite, and cable networks, shared an added value of HKD$7.04 billion. However, the consumption of music in the form of CDs was much reduced (Fung, 2013), whereas Hong Kong's film industry was still at its nadir (Chan, Fung, & Ng, 2009).

The only considerable portion of the creative industries that could be included in this analysis is the information industry, in which the publishing sector—including printing, publishing, and retailing activities related to books, newspapers, and magazines—is an important element of these services in Hong Kong. During the last sixty years, in response to societal changes, important newspapers have been established to fulfill the information needs of the people of Hong Kong, at first for understanding communist China and then later for practical purposes. Established in the 1950s, *Ming Pao* responded to social needs during the rapid increase in Hong Kong's population due to a large influx of Chinese immigrants exiled from China until 1974 when the Touch Base policy for immigrants was terminated. The *Hong Kong Economic Journal*, which was founded in the 1970s, was a direct result of Hong Kong's developing financial and property estate market. In the 1990s, the liberal and democratic *Apple Daily* responded to political needs when the people of Hong Kong were stunned by the Tiananmen Square protests of 1989 (Tang, Cheng, & So, 2014). Recently, however, a "free model" of newspapers and online newspapers has strongly eroded the readership of daily newspapers (So, 2009). Readers' gradual switch to online reporting also further curtailed the distribution of these newspapers. By 2012, the value added of this industry had shrunk to HKD$14.07 billion. The advertising industry operates in tandem with the mass media. In 2012, the value added of advertising was HKD$7.32 billion (Hong Kong Census and Statistics Department, 2014a).

Smaller creative industries, including design (e.g., interior decoration and furniture design, multimedia design, visual design, and graphic design), had an added value of HKD$3.31 billion. The architecture industry comprises city planning, architectural design, and other activities related to architecture and urban landscaping. Because Hong Kong is an international, cosmopolitan city, urban planning and landscaping are vital, and in recent years, regional development and the construction of infrastructure have brought opportunities to the architecture industry. In 2012, the value added of this industry was HKD$9.26 billion. Amusement services include amusement parks, theme parks, and game centers, but these are a relatively small component of Hong Kong's creative industries. In 2012, the value added of amusement services was HKD$1.89 billion.

Of relevance to the game industry is SCGIM. This sector includes the publishing and distribution of computer software and computer games, in addition to the Internet and other telecommunication activities; data processing; and web portals. In 2012, the value added of this industry was

HKD$37.76 billion, nearly ten times the value added of the film, video, and music industry.

DEVELOPMENT OF HONG KONG'S CREATIVE INDUSTRIES

The HKSAR gauges the development of its industries in terms of the employment opportunities created and the volume of trade in relevant products and services. As noted in the last section, our value-added statistics were derived mainly from data collected through the Annual Survey of Economic Activities (ASEA). Employment statistics are based on data collected by the Quarterly Survey of Employment and Vacancies. The labor force employed in the creative industries includes full-time employees, part-time employees, working directors, proprietors, partners, and family workers. The trade statistics of cultural and creative products are based on data collected from declarations of imports and exports. The statistics of cultural and creative services are based on data collected by annual surveys of imports and exports of service (Hong Kong Census and Statistics Department, 2014a).

Based on these estimates, from 2005 to 2012, the cultural and creative industries in Hong Kong showed an increasing trend. In 2005, the total value added was HKD$52.26 billion. In 2006, it had reached HKD$57.31 billion, an increase of 9.67 percent. In 2007, it was HKD$65.12 billion, an increase of 13.62 percent. In 2008, the global financial crisis drastically decreased the economic environment of Hong Kong, including that of the creative indus-

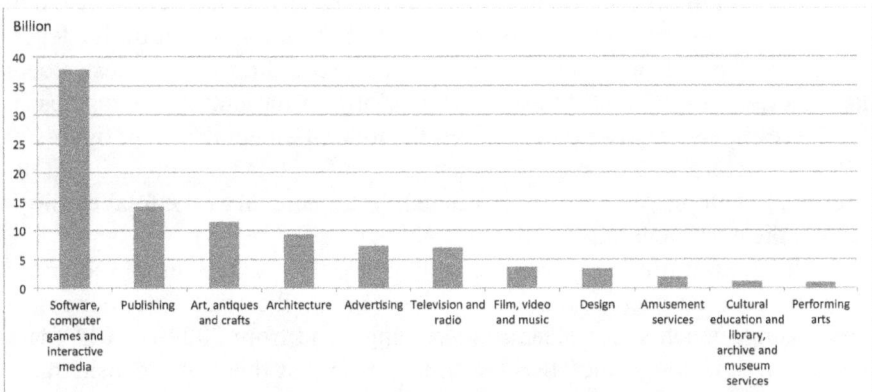

Figure 2.1.   Value Added of Different Sectors of the Hong Kong Cultural Industries in 2012. *Sources*: This chart was created by the author based on data sources from government statistics about the cultural and creative industries in Hong Kong.

tries. In 2008 and 2009, the growth rate showed signs of slowing down, and the annual value added was reduced to a level lower than that of 2007. However, in 2009, Hong Kong's creative industries rebounded, reaching a value added of HKD$77.57 billion, an increase of 22.61 percent. In 2012, the statistics showed that the value added of the creative industries was HKD$97.83 billion, an increase of 87.20 percent over the value added in 2005.

The proportion of the value added of the creative industries in the total GDP also increased. In 2005, the value added of the creative industries contributed to 38 percent of total GDP. This percentage grew to 4.9 percent in 2012 (see figure 2.2). Based on these figures, the HKSAR claimed the importance of the creative industries. Their relevance to Hong Kong has been shown to increase. From 2005 to 2012, the three most prosperous sectors in Hong Kong's creative industries were SCGIM; art, antiques, and crafts; and architecture. The increases in the value added of these three sectors were HKD$21.25 billion, HKD$7.22 billion, and HKD$6.10 billion, respectively. These amounts show that the game industry is at the very core of the creative industries and is the fastest growing. Nevertheless, the contribution of the creative industries to the entire economy was not significant, given that in 2014, the global average was 7 percent and that the UK, the industry leader, reported only 7.9 percent (Zuhdi, 2014). As mentioned earlier, in order to provide a realistic view of the content of the industries, I argue that the contribution of the creative industries to Hong Kong's economy is not as huge as it has been suggested. Furthermore, if the actual output produced in relation to creative or cultural products such as films, animations, and music were tallied, the percentage would be less (Zuhdi, 2014).

In addition to the increased value added of these sectors, the expansion in employment has been referred to as another important indicator of the development of Hong Kong's creative industries. According to the most recent data, more than 200,000 people were working in the cultural industries in 2012 (see figure 2.3). Figure 2.4 shows the total of all employment figures in different sectors of the creative industries. The SCGIM sector included almost 50,000 employees, which accounted for 25 percent of the total employment in the creative industries in Hong Kong (see figure 2.4).

In 2012, according to government statistics, the workers in all sectors of the creative industries constituted 5.5 percent of the total employment in Hong Kong, which was a steadily increasing trend from 2008 to 2011 (data not shown). Although the HKSAR could argue that there was considerable room for development in the future, it could also be argued that in this period, only a small proportion of the work force in Hong Kong was involved in the creative industries.

From 2005 to 2012, the data showed variances in the number of workers engaged in different sectors of the cultural industries. In some rising sectors,

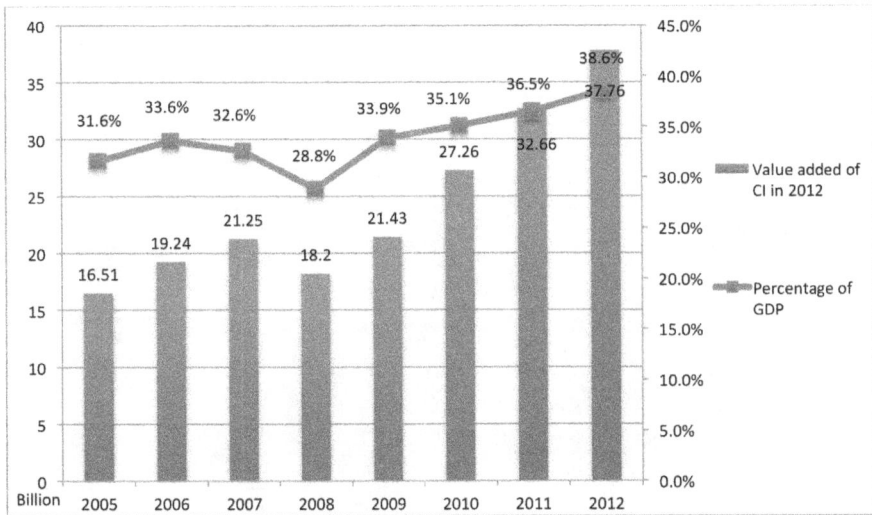

Figure 2.2. Value Added of the Cultural Industries from 2005 to 2012. *Sources:* This chart was created by the author based on data sources from government statistics about the cultural and creative industries in Hong Kong.

such as SCGIM, the number of employees increased by about 10,000, an increase of 24.5 percent. However, in other sectors, the number of employees decreased. For instance, the number of workers in the publishing industry was 47,010 in 2005, which had declined to 44,220 by 2012, while the number of workers in television and radio was 7,350 in 2005, which had declined to 5,730 by 2012 (see figure 2.4). Inevitably, the development of new technology and the rise of new media had a great impact on the traditional media and publishing industries. The change in the number of employees in the above industries is one indicator of this influence.

Compared to the total population in the East Asian region, the local Hong Kong market is relatively small, which is to Hong Kong's disadvantage. One key to Hong Kong's success is its exports to the enormous Chinese market and its long service as China's entrepôt for the global market. However, Hong Kong is overly dependent on the Chinese market, a dependency that has shifted from trade and business to a social condition in which all Hong Kong's daily needs, including food and water, are imported from China.

With regard to the creative industries, at present Hong Kong's dependence on China would seem minimal if only movies, television, popular songs, and games were taken into account. In formal governmental records, there is no particular mention of the volume of import and export of cultural industries from and to China. In development of cultural industries, the total

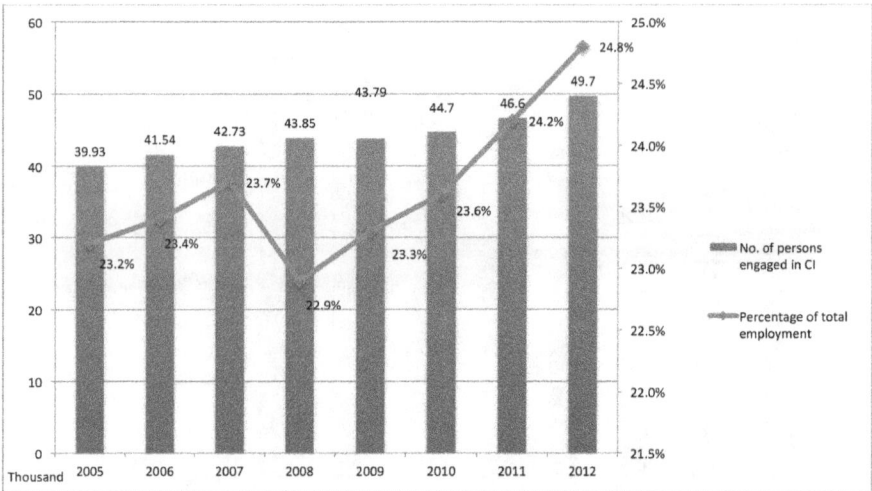

Figure 2.3.   Number of Persons Engaged in the Cultural Industries from 2005 to 2012. *Sources:* **This chart was created by the author based on data sources from government statistics about the cultural and creative industries in Hong Kong.**

number of exports and imports is always a key measurement. From 2005 to 2012, the global exports of cultural and creative goods increased from HKD$422.37 billion to HKD$537.87 billion, and the exports of cultural and creative services increased from HKD$13.63 billion to HKD$25.92 billion. However, the percentage of total exports that are cultural goods and services has decreased slightly in the last few years. The export of cultural and creative goods comprised 18.8 percent of total exports of goods in 2005 but decreased to 15.7 percent in 2012. Similarly, the export of cultural and creative services was 3.7 percent of the total export of services, which decreased to 3.4 percent in 2012. If Hong Kong's core creative industries depend on exportation, these figures illustrate a gloomy picture for Hong Kong's economy.

Imports of cultural and creative goods and services increased from 2005 to 2012, which indicated a growing demand for creative and cultural products and services in Hong Kong. In 2005, the import of cultural and creative goods was HKD$357.41 billion, or 15.3 percent of the total number of imports. In 2012, the imports increased to HKD$609.62 billion, or 15.6 percent of the total number of imports. The importation of cultural and creative services increased from HKD$15.6 billion in 2005 to HKD$25.34 billion in 2012. The percentage of the total number of imports of services increased slightly from 3.6 percent in 2005 to 4.3 percent in 2012 (Hong Kong Census and Statistics Department, 2014a).

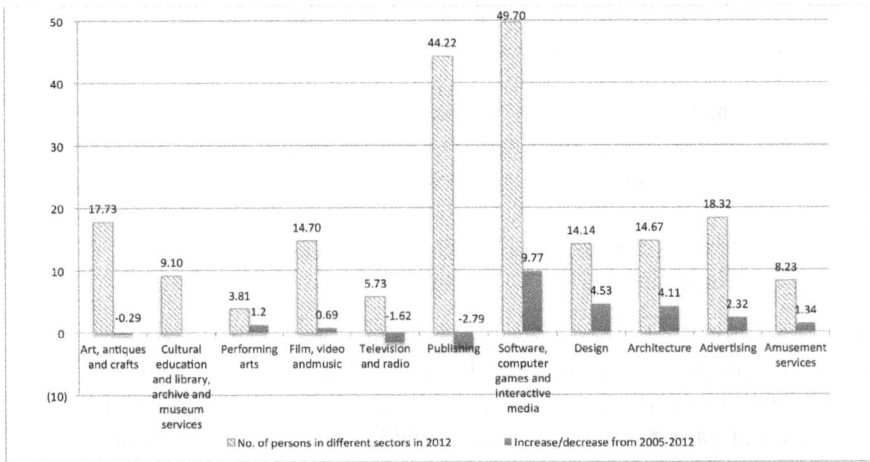

Figure 2.4.   Number of Persons Engaged in Different Sectors of the Cultural Industries from 2005 to 2012. *Sources*: **This chart was created by the author based on data sources from government statistics about the cultural and creative industries in Hong Kong.**

From 2005 to 2012, the statistical data showed a trend in the increasing development of Hong Kong's cultural industries. The value added of the cultural and creative industries increased steadily, which indicated their vibrancy during this period. The number of workers engaged in the cultural and creative industries also increased, which indicates that the cultural industries attracted a larger number of talented employees. The export and import of cultural and creative goods and services also increased, which indicated higher competitiveness and a robust demand for cultural and creative goods and services.

Among the cultural industries in Hong Kong, the SCGIM industry, especially the game sector, has experienced the most rapid development. In the next section, the characteristics of Hong Kong's game industry will be discussed and compared with those of other sectors in the creative industries in the HKSAR.

THE HONG KONG GAME INDUSTRY IN HONG KONG'S CREATIVE AND CULTURAL INDUSTRIES

As I've noted, Hong Kong's creative industries include eleven sectors. The most rapidly expanding is SCGIM. From 2005 to 2012, the value added of this sector increased from HKD$16.51 billion to HKD$37.76 billion, an increase of 128.7 percent. The employment market for this industry also grew. The number of workers in this industry increased from 39,930 in 2005 to 49,700 in 2012, an increase of 24.5 percent. The game sector, which is a prominent domain in this industry, plays a significant role in Hong Kong's creative industries. In the following section, the characteristics of the game sector and other new subsectors in the creative industries will be compared before we consider the context of Hong Kong's creative industries and compare the development of different sectors.

Characteristics of Subsectors of Hong Kong's New Creative Industries

The game industry, video games in particular, is a rising domain in Hong Kong. Video games are usually electronic games that involve interaction between the user and a user interface. In video games, visual feedback given to the user or gamer is generated by a video device. In different platforms of visual feedback, video games are categorized as either "console games" or "computer games." Console games consist of gamer-controlled images and the sounds generated by a video game console through a television monitor or other audiovisual system. Examples of game consoles are Sony's PlayStation and the Nintendo Wii. Computer games, which are also called personal computer (PC) games, are video games played on a PC instead of a game console.

Tschang (2009) analyzed the four basic characteristics of the game industry and compared different subsectors of Hong Kong's creative industries, including games, animation, computer graphics, virtual worlds, social networking sites, and design. First, the main components of the video game industry are Internet technology (i.e., gaming technologies) and content (i.e., art and animation). Thus, the game industry requires workers who are talented both technologically and artistically in producing animation.

Second, in video games the form of user interaction is active, whereas the form of user interaction in animation and computer graphics is passive. Hence, the development of video games must focus on the user's interaction experience via a computer or console.

Third, the user's objective in playing video games is to be challenged and to socialize. Players gain satisfaction by winning games or gaining passes in games. By collaborating with other players, users also benefit from the socialization aspect of gaming. In this era of the Internet, with the exception of a few standalone PC games, almost all popular games are online, which is the focus of this book. In a massively multiplayer online role-playing game (MMORPG), users assume a specific character or role in the gameplay or game world with which they interact with other gamers online. MMORPGs in the period of this study were considered the most popular and profitable online game (they have now been replaced by mobile games). In the gaming process, gamers derive enjoyment not only from the exhilaration of the challenge and mission of the roles they play but also from the process of socialization and communication that takes place during the competition, collaboration, collective missions and tasks, chats, and so forth offered by each specific game design. The uniqueness of this gratification is the reason that it entices gamers to pay both directly for games and indirectly for products related to those games, and it also explains why this particular industry has expanded more rapidly than other creative industries have, such as the animation, computer graphics, and design industries.

Tschang's fourth basic characteristic of the game industry is that the objectives of both businesses and consumers include products and services. Thus game companies can provide both. As do game companies, animation companies provide both products and services, whereas computer graphics and design companies are usually service providers only.

A COMPARISON OF GAME INDUSTRIES AND OTHER SECTORS OF THE CREATIVE AND CULTURAL INDUSTRIES

The statistics examined in this study revealed that some sectors in the creative and cultural industries grew faster than other sectors during the preceding decade (Hong Kong Census and Statistics Department, 2014a). The game industry is clearly one of the most rapidly growing creative industries. In this study, particular attention was paid to data on the development of cultural and creative industries in Hong Kong from 2005 to 2012.

In 2005 and 2006, SCGIM, publishing, and television and radio were the three largest sectors in terms of annual value added (Hong Kong Census and Statistics Department, 2014a). The value added of these three sectors represented about 70 percent of the total value added in Hong Kong's cultural and creative industries. Beginning in 2007, SCGIM remained the largest sector, while art, antiques, and crafts boomed and became the third-largest sector.

The data show that in 2005, the value added of SCGIM was HKD$16.51 billion and represented 31.6 percent of the total value added of the creative and cultural industries (Hong Kong Census and Statistics Department, 2014a). In 2006, the value added grew to HKD$19.24 billion, which was 33.6 percent of these industries. In 2007, the value added increased to HKD$21.25 billion, but the percentage decreased slightly to 32.6 percent. In 2008, the economy in Hong Kong was in recession, which negatively affected the creative industries, and as part of the cultural industries, the SCGIM industry was greatly affected. The value added of this industry fell to HKD$18.20 billion in 2008 or 14.3 percent. It represented only 28.8 percent of the total value added of the cultural and creative industries. The economy in Hong Kong began to recover in 2009. Hence, the value added of the

SCGIM industry also increased. In 2012, the value added of this industry reached HKD$37.76 billion, which was 38.6 percent of the total value added of all cultural industries (see figure 2.5). This sector remains the pillar of Hong Kong's cultural and creative industries.

The employment data also showed that SCGIM was Hong Kong's largest and fastest growing sector. In 2005, the number of workers in this sector was the second largest of all sectors of the cultural and creative industries (39,930 persons). In that year, publishing was the largest sector, employing 47,010 persons. Art, antiques, and crafts were the third-largest sector in terms of the size of the labor force (18,020 persons). The number of workers in the above three sectors was 61.0 percent of the total number of those working in Hong Kong's cultural and creative industries.

From 2005 to 2012, the employment market in the cultural and creative industries in Hong Kong was generally attractive. The number of workers in the SCGIM sector increased from 2005 to 2007. In 2005, 2006, and 2007, the number of workers in this industry accounted for 23.2 percent, 23.4 percent and 23.7 percent, respectively, of the total number of workers in the cultural and creative industries. Then there was a short period of decline in 2008 when the number fell to 22.9 percent because of the overall economic downturn. However, the job market did not continue to shrink. In 2009 it began to

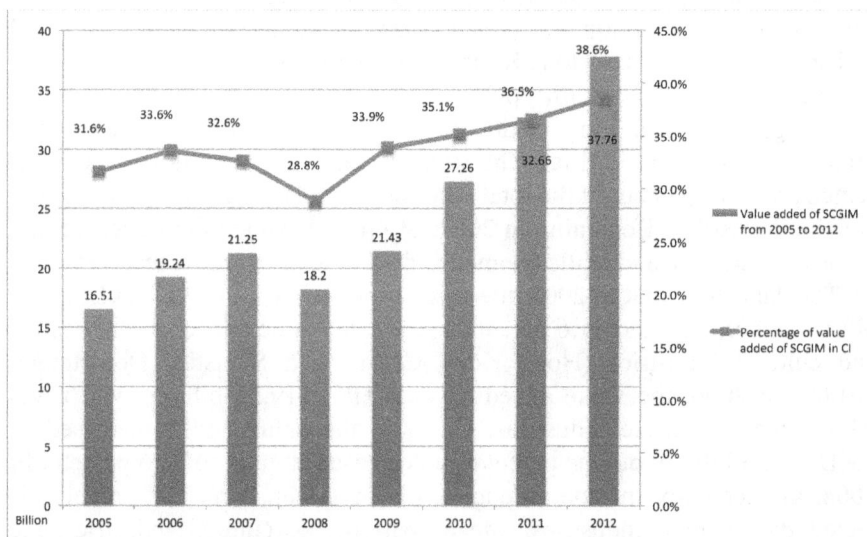

Figure 2.5. Value Added of Software, Computer Games, and Interactive Media (SCGIM) from 2005 to 2012. *Sources:* This chart was created by the author based on data sources from government statistics about the cultural and creative industries in Hong Kong.

expand, and by 2011 it had become Hong Kong's largest sector. In 2012, the number of workers in SCGIM reached 49,700, which represented 24.8 percent of the total number of workers in the cultural industries. In this relatively new economy, this specific industry expanded rapidly, whereas the job markets in some traditional industries diminished. For example, in 2005, the number of workers in television and radio was 7,350 (4.3 percent), which decreased to 5,730 (2.9 percent) in 2012. Similarly, the number of workers in publishing was 47,010 (27.3 percent) in 2005, and this decreased to 44,220 (22.1 percent) in 2012 (see figure 2.6).

In short, in the context of Hong Kong's cultural and creative industries, the game industry is booming. During the last few years, it has become evident that the game industry has created economic benefits for Hong Kong and has added job opportunities for the local labor force. It seems that this trend will continue. In the next section, I'll examine Hong Kong's game industry in detail.

OVERVIEW OF HONG KONG'S GAME INDUSTRY

There are more than 7.8 million residences in Hong Kong, of which more than 2.24 million have access to broadband (Cheng, 2012). This has provided the background for the development of Hong Kong's game industry.

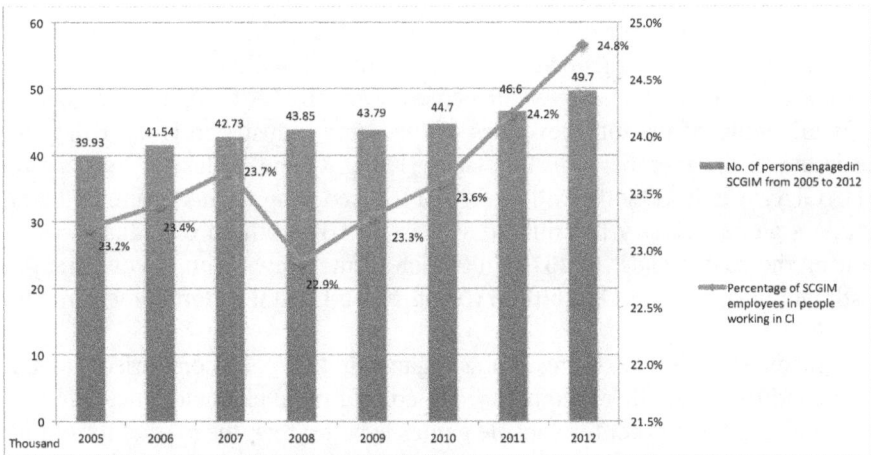

Figure 2.6. Number of Persons Engaged in Software, Computer Games, and Interactive Media (SCGIM) from 2005 to 2012. *Sources:* **This chart was created by the author based on data sources from government statistics about the cultural and creative industries in Hong Kong.**

Because of the geographic proximity and common language of Hong Kong and Macau, their game industries are usually discussed in combination. Moreover, Macau's online gaming is a branch of Hong Kong's game industry. The total number of residences in Hong Kong and Macau is about 8.07 million. Taiwan is another important traditional Chinese market. The total number of residences in Taiwan is about 23.16 million. The ratio of residences in Hong Kong and Macau to those in Taiwan is 1 to 3. In 2010, the market for online games in Hong Kong and Macau was RMB¥0.15 billion, while the market in Taiwan was NT$12.57 billion (about RMB¥2.68 billion). The ratio of market sizes in Hong Kong and Macau to those in Taiwan was 1 to 19, which was far less than the ratio of the total number of residences.

In addition to market size, the number of listed companies in Hong Kong and Macau is also far less than in Taiwan. In 2010, nine game companies were publicly incorporated in Taiwan, including Chinese Gamer, Wayi Entertainment, International Game System, User Joy, Oh My God, Soft-World International Entertainment, Soft Star, InterServ International, and Gamania, whereas no Hong Kong local game company was listed that year. In 2016, in Taiwan, the number of publicly listed companies increased to fourteen, and in Hong Kong, the first local game company, Gameone Group, was publicly incorporated in the Growth Enterprise Market, which is an alternative stock market in Hong Kong (see figure 2.7).

Hence, there is much room for the further development of the game industry in Hong Kong and Macau. Based on the population ratio and the average revenue per unit (ARPU) value (which corresponds to Hong Kong's consumption level), it has been estimated that about RMB¥0.7 billion of the game market in Hong Kong is undeveloped. In the interviews we conducted in 2013, the owners of game companies estimated that the growth rate of the online game market was over 30 percent annually. Although there was no official figure of the total revenues of the game industry in Hong Kong, an estimate from members of the Hong Kong Game Industry Association (HKGIA) was HKD$600 million in 2011. According to this estimate, Hong Kong's game industry has missed at least RMB¥2 billion of industry value during the past decade. In 2017, in the latest interviews with the owners, the estimate was over HKD$1 billion (Hong Kong Digital Entertainment Industry, 2017).

An examination of Hong Kong's game industry in comparison to the game industries in other countries revealed four main characteristics. First, in Hong Kong, the market for console games is better than the market for online games, just as in the United States and Japan, console games dominate the game market. As an international, cosmopolitan city, Hong Kong is sensitive to Asian and overseas trends, and it is particularly susceptible to the influence of the United States and Japan. Thus the market for console games in Hong Kong has always followed these markets. As these markets performed

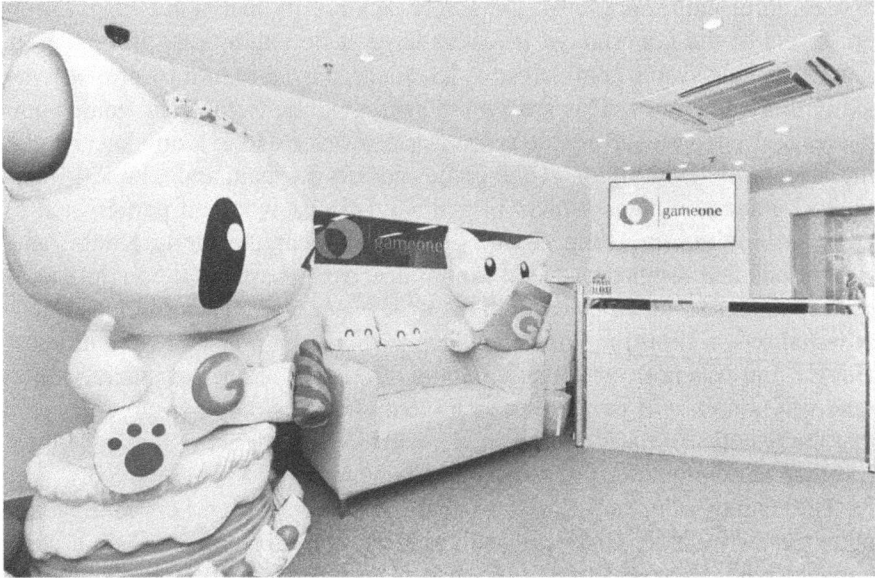

Figure 2.7.   Gameone Main Office in Hong Kong

well, so did Hong Kong's. In addition to the influence of game markets overseas, strict restrictions on importing game consoles from mainland China has shielded Hong Kong from the Chinese market. Compared with console games, in Hong Kong online games are underdeveloped, although they are progressing. Specifically, the online games market has been impeded by inconvenient channels of payment, the absence of a promotion policy, the high cost of human resources, a shortage of game development and operation companies, and a lack of government support. Thus the market for games in Hong Kong has much room for improvement.

Second, Hong Kong's game industry integrates the resources of other relevant industries (the entertainment industry for example) and uses their advantages. Business operations in Hong Kong's entertainment industry are mature, and the cultural elements of the entertainment industry are well developed. In addition, the cultural icons of the entertainment industry are well known by the mainland Chinese audience, which serves to attract attention and investment from mainland China. In Hong Kong's game industry, some companies collaborate with game companies on the Chinese mainland and develop game products related to famous Hong Kong movies (e.g., *Teddy Boys*) and television dramas (e.g., different *wuxia* games, *wuxia* being a genre focused on martial artists in ancient China).

   Third, the trade flows of Hong Kong's game industry are relatively slow, and communication platforms are sorely lacking. In mainland China, different levels of the government invest in large-scale exhibitions of animation, games, and electronic commerce, which are organized in turn by professional exhibition companies. This strategy increases publicity for local game companies and integrates available resources. However, Hong Kong lags behind the large-scale exhibitions of the game industry in mainland China. I interviewed game company owners in mainland China who had participated in game exhibitions in Hong Kong. They stated that the Hong Kong game exhibitions had for them several limitations. For example, although the entrance fees for Hong Kong exhibitions were expensive, the exhibitions usually lasted only a short time. In their view, participating in game exhibitions in Hong Kong was not cost effective. In addition, the number of attendees was relatively small, and publicity was limited. Thus the company owners said that the benefits of participating in game exhibitions in Hong Kong were far less than in other markets (e.g., Shanghai's ChinaJoy).

   The employment statistics show that the number of workers in the computer games industry has increased in recent years. In order to gain a clear picture of the talent structure, a survey was conducted in 2010 to examine the demographics and the characteristics of game talent in Hong Kong. Through the HKGIA, the survey was distributed to around 70 percent of games companies, which included the top five companies in Hong Kong.

   According to the survey, game talent ranged in age from twenty to thirty-six years old. The average age of the respondents was twenty-eight, which indicated that young people were the main force in the game industry. Regarding education level, 49 percent of the employees in game companies had completed high school or below, 30 percent had graduated from college, and 21 percent held a bachelor's degree or higher. Although the amount of game talent with higher education was increasing, these workers were still not in the majority. Regarding income, the median monthly salary was HKD$12,400, but monthly salaries were as high as HKD$22,000 in other industries. And based on estimates using interviews conducted in 2017, salaries have not changed much since then. For example, the average relevant monthly salary in Hong Kong in 2010 was less than HKD$11,500, while in 2017, the average salary was around HKD$15,500 (Trading Economics, 2017).

   In support of the game industry, the Hong Kong government has invested labor and resources to develop industry collaboration centers and various university training programs. According to Tschang (2009), the Chinese University of Hong Kong (CUHK), Hong Kong Polytechnic University (PolyU), and the City University of Hong Kong (CityU) provided support for the game industry. CUHK offers two- and three-year undergraduate programs in creative media and a master's program in fine arts. The undergraduate program attracts about eighty students per year. Meanwhile, PolyU is one of the strongest institutions in the design and gaming sectors, and it offers both undergraduate and graduate programs in multimedia and design. It also established a Multimedia Innovation Centre in 1999. PolyU's Game Lab in the Department of Computing focuses on game design and research, offering programs in toy design, public areas design, and Asian lifestyles design. In 2017, PolyU also organized the Chinese Digital Games Research Association (DIGRA) conference, a regional conference of this international association. Tschang (2009) noted that PolyU's one-year program for a master of science in multimedia and entertainment technology provided training in both technology and design. Thus graduates were more likely to work in the areas of video games and online entertainment, 2-D and 3-D animation, and digital video and special effects. The program is similar to that of the world-famous Center for Entertainment Technology Master Program at Carnegie Mellon University. Although it is not easy to manage a program like this effectively in a small, local market, PolyU is still willing to invest in the program, and it is optimistic about its prospects for developing game talent.

In addition to these universities, the Institute of Vocational Education and Hong Kong Art School also offered programs in art and animation and video game design. Tschang (2009) concluded that there was not a significant lack of game talent in Hong Kong. However, the problem was that these programs focused on basic skills rather than advanced training. Tschang found that although a substantial amount of talent was fostered by these institutions and programs, they needed to improve their ability to meet the requirements of the game industry.

In addition to investment in educational resources, the Hong Kong government has also established preferential policies for the online game industry. Supplement VII of the *Mainland China and Hong Kong Closer Economic Partnership Arrangement* (*CEPA*; Hong Kong Trade and Industry Department, 2010) allows service suppliers in Hong Kong to establish "Internet culture business units and Internet online service business premises in the mainland in the form of contractual joint ventures with the mainland party holding dominant interests." Supplement VI of the *CEPA* (Hong Kong Trade and Industry Department, 2010) states in addition that "the time limit for completion of the examination of contents (including examination conducted by experts) of imported online game products developed by Hong Kong shall be two months, subject to provision of full supporting documents."

The Hong Kong government has provided funds to support the creative industries, especially the game industry. In 2009, the government provided HKD$300 million to establish Create Hong Kong (CreateHK), an office dedicated to promoting the development of creative industries. The office was established under the Communications and Technology Branch of the Commerce and Economic Development Bureau (Hong Kong Information

Services Department, 2013). Sze Yan Ngai, convener of HKGIA, was invited to become a committee member of CreateHK. In 2010, CreateHK provided HKD$4 million to sponsor the Asia Online Game Awards, receiving support from nine Asian areas: mainland China, Taiwan, Korea, the Philippines, Vietnam, Thailand, Malaysia, Hong Kong, and Singapore. The event aims at making Hong Kong the trading platform of the Asian game industry. In addition, the HKSAR also sponsors various annual events, such as the Asian Game Show (with HKGIA) and the ANI-COM exhibition (with the Hong Kong Comics and the Animation Federation).

Government officials have shown support for Hong Kong's game industry. In a speech, Donald Tsang, former chief executive of the HKSAR, reiterated that the cultural industry was one of the six dominant industries in Hong Kong. In 2009, Donald Tsang visited Gameone Group, one of the most prominent local game companies. His visit symbolized the government's support of the industry.

MAPPING HONG KONG'S GAME MARKET

In 2006, the global intelligence and market data company International Data Corporation (IDC) estimated that the online gaming market in Hong Kong was US$30.6 million (2007). This number increased in the next few years. Tschang (2009) argued that the gaming market had one of the three highest growth markets in Hong Kong.

To review, according to a survey conducted by HKGIA in 2009, the total revenue of the Hong Kong online gaming market was HKD$520 million. It was estimated to reach HKD$630 million in 2010 and HKD$700 million in 2011. Our research team conducted a survey in 2010, and the results showed that the market size of online gaming in Hong Kong was about HKD$650 million, an increase of HKD$130 million. Although the growth was higher than the estimate, it constituted a very small part (0.03 percent) of total GDP. In 2010, there were thirty-six game companies of a substantial scale in Hong Kong. The cost of the investment of the companies was as high as HKD$132 million.

In 2010, the top five Hong Kong game companies were Gamania Digital Entertainment, Gameone Interactive, Chinese Gamer International, Game-First International, and GameFlier International (see table 2.1). The top three companies were established in 2000, and their main business now includes server operation, game research and development (R&D), and game publishing. These three companies have different strategies for market positioning. Gamania is a branch of a Taiwan-listed company in Hong Kong. The major advantage of this company is the diversity of its products. It publishes many Korean games such as *Dragon Nest* (龍之谷) and *Counter Striker Online* (絕

Table 2.1.   Top Five Online Game Companies in Hong Kong in 2010

No.	Company Name	Established	Main Business
1	Gamania Digital Entertainment 遊戲橘子	June 2000	Game server operator in Hong Kong with some game servers in Taiwan
2	Gameone Interactive.com Inc. 智傲控股	July 2000	Media publisher, game developer, and game publisher
3	Chinese Gamer International Corp. 中華網龍	March 2000	Involved in online game research and development and operating services
4	GameFirst International Corp. 智凡迪	March 2005	Publisher of several famous games, including *World of Warcraft*, *StarCraft II*, and *Diablo III*.
5	GameFlier International Corp. 遊戲新幹線	July 2002	Game publisher

對武力). Gameone Group is a typical local game company, and it successfully integrates R&D and media. The main business of this company is operating game products developed by mainland Chinese companies. Chinese Gamer is a branch of the largest Taiwan R&D game company in Hong Kong. It launches four or five independently developed games every year. The major theme of the games is martial arts (武俠), and most of the games are adapted from novels and comics, such as *Tian Zi Chuan Qi Online* (天子傳奇Online) and *Huang Yi Qun Xia Zhuan 2* (黃易群俠傳2). The other two companies, GameFirst and GameFlier, are mainly game publishers.

Regarding total revenue, in 2010, the top five companies contributed about 70 percent of the game market in Hong Kong, which indicates that the market for game R&D and game publishing in Hong Kong is confined to a small number of large game companies. Although the top five companies have been successful in terms of game publishing, the full potential of game R&D has not yet been achieved.

The Internet cafe is an important channel for distribution of online games. About 10 percent of 1 million game players chose to play online games in Internet cafes in 2011. There are 141 Internet cafes in Hong Kong, 28 percent of which belong to I-ONE and 20 percent of which belong to Msystem. Each of these two corporations took 20 percent of the total market revenue in Hong Kong. The remaining 60 percent of the market was held by small

Internet cafes. Students form the majority of the customers of Internet cafes, but professionals are also willing to spend leisure time there. The demographic profiles of the customers of Internet cafes vary in different areas (see figure 2.8).

In July 2011, we conducted a random survey of Internet cafes in Hong Kong. The results showed that 43 percent of customers very often played games in Internet cafes, 45 percent occasionally played games in Internet cafes, and 12 percent seldom played games in Internet cafes. The reasons that Internet cafes have become an important distribution channel of online gaming include their convenience, comfort, and atmosphere as well as their low prices and the opportunity they offer players to socialize with other players (see figure 2.9).

In 2010, we examined the retail market in Hong Kong and Macau, finding that the convenience store 7-Eleven was the largest retailer of game products. The total number of 7-Eleven retail stores in Hong Kong and Macau was 963, which contributed to 37 percent of the total retail market. The second-largest retailer was general game shop. Seventy-seven game shops in Hong Kong and Macau held 27 percent of the total retail market. OK convenience stores were the third-largest retailer. The 313 OK convenience stores held 12

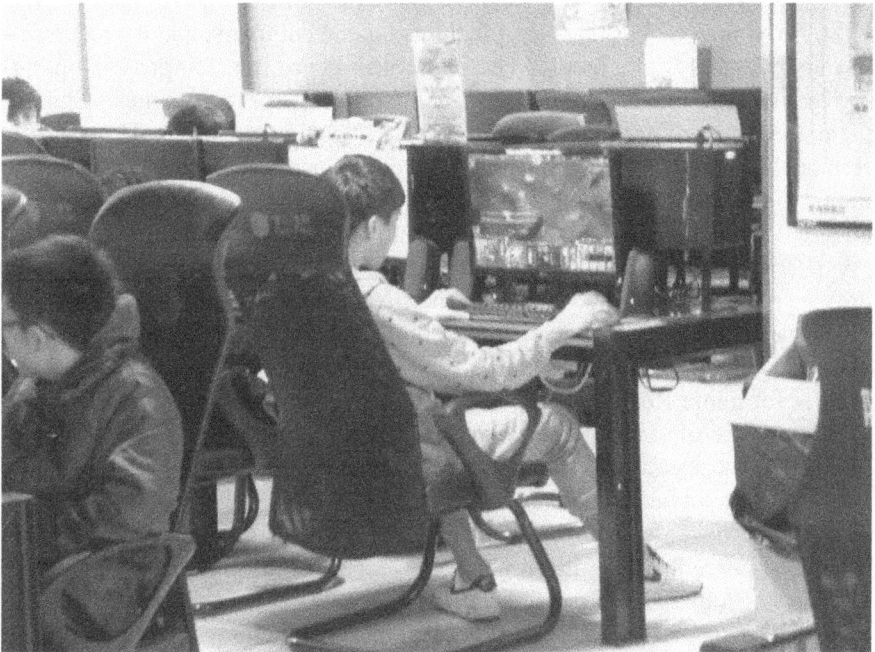

Figure 2.8.   Typical Internet Cafe in Hong Kong

percent of the total retail market, while Epaylinks held 12 percent of the total retail market. Other retailers, including Lee Yuen Subscription Agencies, Now.com.hk, Hong Kong Broadband Network (HKBN), the Mass Transit Railway (MTR), Companhia de Telecomunicações de Macau (CTM), and Ba-bi held about 12 percent of the retail market.

The data gathered from the survey conducted in 2011 showed that convenience stores were the most important retail vendors of online game products to Internet-cafe players. The survey showed that 82 percent of the respondents bought point cards in convenience stores, while 22.4 percent of the respondents bought point cards in game shops. Epaylinks, HKBN, and other retail channels held a very small part of the total market.

By 2012, the proportions of the retail market had changed. According to an industrial report on the 2012 Asia Online Game Summit (Cheng, 2012), the 1,300 convenience stores in Hong Kong then held 50 percent of the retail market, the proportion of Epaylinks had increased significantly from 12 percent to 25 percent. The game shops shared a substantial proportion of the retail market, but fifty game shops constituted only 15 percent of the total retail market. Other channels held 10 percent of the total market.

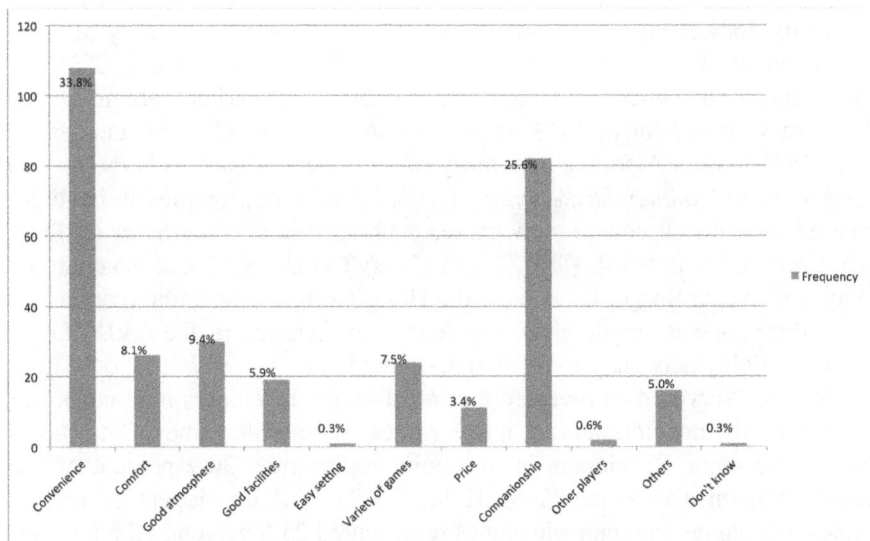

Figure 2.9.   Reasons for Playing Games in Internet Cafes

THE MOST POPULAR GAMES IN THE
HONG KONG GAME MARKET

Based on market share in 2010, we found that most game players in Hong Kong (77 percent) viewed role-playing games (RPG) favorably. The number of gamers who were interested in casual games (16 percent) and browser games (7 percent) was relatively small. The empirical data collected in 2011 also showed that over half of Internet-cafe gamers under twenty-five years old preferred RPG or shooter games, whereas over half of Internet-cafe gamers under twenty-five years old did not like playing Mahjong or educational games (Fung, 2013).

The data gathered in 2012 showed that client games accounted for 83 percent of the market share, browser games held 15 percent of the market share, and mobile phone games had only 2 percent of the market share (Cheng, 2012). Although the proportion of mobile games was limited in 2012, there was a clear indication that mobile games would play an increasingly important role in the game market because of the development and popularization of smart phones.

Based on the data on the four major game media in 2010, including 2000 fun, Nakuz, *PC Game Weekly*, and *G-Zone*, we compiled a list of the ten most popular online games in Hong Kong and Macau (see table 2.2).

In recent years, Google has made an annual announcement that indicates the trend in keywords most frequently used in Google searches. Although game-searching activities are influenced by many factors such as the age of the game and which search engine is used, the top ten most searched for games in Hong Kong can be seen as an indication of the popularity of these online games. When comparing the 2012 and 2013 lists (see table 2.3), we found that some games that were popular in 2012 and earlier were no longer the most searched for in 2013, such as *Diablo 3* (暗黑破壞神3) and *Angry Birds* (憤怒小鳥). Also, the popularity of other games, such as *San Guo Sha* (三國殺) and *Counter Strike Online* (絕對武力Online), seemed to have decreased as well. Of course, new games such as *Puzzle & Dragons* (龍族拼圖), *Chain Chronicle* (鎖鏈戰記), and *Candy Crush* (糖果大爆險) continue to appear. According to these lists, the Hong Kong online game market is a very vibrant one as the old gives way to the new. Therefore, the R&D of new games is highly necessary to fulfill market demand.

Previous survey data revealed that most game developers in Hong Kong focused on the development of online games and mobile games. Data shows that online game developers at one point represented 30.9 percent of the game companies in Hong Kong (IDC, 2007). The developers of mobile games, PC games, and console games represented 25.5 percent, 12.6 percent, and 4.4 percent of the total game companies, respectively.

Table 2.2.   Top Ten Most Popular Games in Hong Kong and Macau in 2010

Game	Developer/Publisher
World of Warcraft 魔獸世界	GameFirst
Frontier Online 魔物獵人Online	GameFlier
Tian Long Ba Bu Online 天龍八部 Online	Gameone
Counter Strike Online 絕對武力Online	Gamania
Dragon Nest 龍之谷	Gamania
Fantasy Earth Zero 幻想戰記	Gamania
Talesrunner (TR) 跑Online	Funtown
Zhong Hua Ying Xiong Online 中華英雄Online	Chinese Gamer
SD Gundam Online SD 高達Online	Gameone
Seal Online 夢之希望	GameCyber

The data also showed that the market environment was changing. Several companies focused on mobile phone games and then exited the industry. Because of low barriers to entry, these companies were early developers of mobile games. However, at a certain point, perhaps around 2012, Hong Kong's limited market could not support the increasing numbers of mobile game developers, and the price competition became increasingly intense. Under these circumstances, some companies dropped out of the competition and others changed to developing online games, which mirrored a worldwide trend that had started several years earlier (Tschang, 2009). Further, as smart-phone and mobile devices became more popular, the development of mobile games overtook the trend of developing online games.

Unlike technological products and consumer products, game products can be highly culturally situated. Therefore the local market can be a game's most important target. Game products aimed at local markets are also the most likely to satisfy the consumers of those markets. However, because of the small size of and high competition in these local markets, some game companies in Hong Kong have sought to explore the mainland Chinese and overseas game markets.

Table 2.3.   Top Ten Most Searched For Online Games

Rank	2012	2013
1	*League of Legends* 英雄聯盟	*Puzzle & Dragons* 龍族拼圖
2	*Diablo 3* 暗黑破壞神3	*League of Legends* 英雄聯盟
3	*Minecraft* 當個創世神	*Minecraft* 當個創世神
4	*San G uo S ha* 三國殺	*Chain Chronicle* 鎖鏈戰記
5	*Counter Strike Online* 絕對武力 Online	*Candy Crush* 糖果大爆險
6	*Sleeping Dogs* 香港秘密警察	*Against War* 逆轉三國
7	Angry Birds 憤怒小鳥	San Guo Sha 三國殺
8	*Pokémon* 神奇寶貝	*Fantasy Frontier Online* 幻想神域
9	*Sword Art Online* 刀劍神域	*Tower of Saviors* 神魔之塔
10	*Talesrunner (TR)* 跑Online	*Counter Strike Online* 絕對武力 Online

The mainland Chinese game market is large in terms of number of game players, capital, and investment. It is also vibrant and prosperous because it is a new, rising industry in China. Moreover, mainland Chinese consumers are familiar with and fond of Hong Kong culture, which is indicated by the success of the Hong Kong movie industry in the mainland Chinese market. This popularity lays the foundation for the entry of Hong Kong's game industry into the market in mainland China. However, entrance into this market has not been seen as an easy task because it involves several factors, including adequate capital, advanced technology, and an understanding of Chinese policies. In order to effectively enter this market, Hong Kong's game companies tend to collaborate with Chinese enterprises. This strategic arrangement helps Hong Kong companies find distribution channels, handle cultural differences, and cope with changing policies. Therefore, the question of whether Hong Kong game companies can successfully exploit the mainland market depends equally on the capability of their partners.

Another difficulty in entering the mainland market is the increasing number of strong competitors in China. During the last decade, some mainland game companies have become giants—such as Tencent Games, NetEase

Games, Shanda Games, and Perfect World, which both develop and publish games. In 2012, the total market revenue of the top three game companies in China was RMB¥34.7 billion. Furthermore, research has suggested that moving to China to work is still difficult for Hong Kong's creative workers (Chow, 2017).

In addition, policies and regulations in China present challenges to game companies that try to enter or have already entered the mainland market. When the government's rules change, game companies in Hong Kong must work with the regulatory agencies and adjust their products (Tschang, 2009).

HONG KONG'S GAME INDUSTRIES: WHOSE HOPE?

I began with a general introduction to the creative industries in Hong Kong and then analyzed their development during the past few years. The HKSAR government has conducted an extensive survey of Hong Kong's creative industries. The combined revenues of the eleven industries defined by the government indicated positive growth of the creative industries. However, careful examination of the data shows that the HKSAR's broad definition of "creative industries" actually included many strong, conventional trade sectors in Hong Kong that should not be considered creative industries as they are commonly defined. In brief, the government's broad definition allowed for exaggeration of the scale and scope of the creative industries in Hong Kong. This is evidence that the HKSAR has attempted to manipulate the public discourse on creative industries in Hong Kong by subtly suggesting that Hong Kong lags behind its rivals, thereby justifying the authorities' policy of intervention. Further, alternative voices are seldom heard in Hong Kong society, whereas the official discourse is reiterated in official public speeches and policy addresses. Nonetheless, in the HKSAR, no specific cultural policy exists designed to bolster the creative industries in addition to the game industry.

However, it is fair to say that the survey conducted by the HKSAR found that among the eleven sectors of the creative industries defined by the government, software, computer games, and interactive media had experienced steady development. The survey results also confirmed the value-added advantages of the creative industries. In addition to the amount of revenue generated, the large number of workers employed in Hong Kong's creative industries was beneficial to its economy.

Interpreted in light of the results of this government survey, the findings of my empirical analysis lead to some conclusions about the game industry. First, while the findings have demonstrated that the game industry in Hong Kong holds several advantages for Hong Kong, the creative industries face many challenges such as lack of talent, a small game market, and a lack of concrete governmental support. In the official discourse, the game industry is the pillar of Hong Kong's economic development. However, no concrete effort to support this industry is mentioned in any of the governmental reports examined in this study.

Second, should the government support creative industries? If so, in what ways? These are fundamental questions of political economy. Would it be a backward step if Hong Kong were to adopt a free-market economy? Is it appropriate for the authorities to intervene in the markets of creative industries? Because creative industries involve the production of culture, the issue of cultural politics surmounts the interplay of politics and economics. In other words, there is always the possibility that the ideological interests of the state will influence cultural content.

Third, in recent years, Hong Kong's position as a creative city has been threatened by the rise of the creative industries in Korea, which has given rise to the notion of an East Asian rivalry and which is complicated by the omnipotence of China in its sovereignty over Hong Kong. However, the Chinese market may offer a hidden advantage because it has a pool of resources that Hong Kong could draw on to rival its competitors in Asia. Furthermore, Hong Kong's game industry has the potential to develop games in collaboration with mainland Chinese companies to explore opportunities in the global market, which is seen as a hope for the future. Whether this potential is actual or not remains to be found.

REFERENCES

Chan, J., Fung, A., & Ng, C. H. (2009). *Policies for a sustainable development of the film industry*. Hong Kong: Chinese University Press.
Cheng, C. W. (2012). Industry report on the Hong Kong game industry. [香港區產業報告. 亞洲網絡遊戲高峰會]. Report presented at the *2012 Asia Online Game Summit*, Hong Kong.
Chow, Y. F. (2017). Exploring creative class mobility: Hong Kong creative workers in Shanghai and Beijing. *Eurasia Geography and Economics*, 1–25. Retrieved from http://dx.doi.org/10.1080/15387216.2017.1365311.
Fung, A. [馮應謙]. (2013). Youth and online games in Hong Kong [香港青少年與網絡遊戲]. *Journal of Youth Studies* [青年研究學報] *16*(1), 43–55.
Fung, A., & Shum, S. [馮應謙、沈思]. (2012). *Melodic memories: The historical development of music industry in Hong Kong* [悠揚‧憶記：香港音樂工業發展史]. Hong Kong: Subculture Press.
Google. (2012). Google announces 2012 top search keywords: Electronic and information technology sector [Google 宣佈 2012 年香港熱門關鍵字排行榜—電子及資訊科技類別]. Retrieved from http://www.ringhk.com/news2.php?id=6041.
Google. (2013). Google announces 2012 top search keywords [Google 宣佈 2013 年香港熱門關鍵字搜尋排行榜]. Retrieved from https://www.techritual.com/2013/12/18/54831/ .
Hong Kong Census and Statistics Department (2014a). *Hong Kong monthly digest of statistics: Cultural and creative industries in Hong Kong*. Retrieved from http://www.statistics.gov.hk/pub/B71403FB2014XXXXB0100.pdf.
Hong Kong Census and Statistics Department. (2014b). *Population*. Retrieved from http://www.censtatd.gov.hk/hkstat/sub/so20.jsp.

Hong Kong Digital Entertainment Association. (2017) "Hong Kong digital entertainment industry." Hong Kong: Centre for Communication and Public Opinion Survey, Chinese University of Hong Kong.

Hong Kong Information Services Department (2013). *Hong Kong: The facts.* Retrieved from http://www.gov.hk/en/about/abouthk/factsheets/docs/creative_industries.pdf.

Hong Kong Trade and Industry Department. (2010). *Mainland and Hong Kong closer economic agreement and partnership.* Retrieved from http://tid.gov.hk/english/cepa/index.html.

IDC. (2007). Executive summary. *IDC Hong Kong digital entertainment study (2006–2007).*

Kakiuchi, E., & Takeuchi, K. (2014). Creative industries: Reality and potential in Japan. GRIPS discussion paper 14–04. Retrieved from http://www.grips.ac.jp/r-center/wp-content/uploads/14-04.pdf.

So, Y. K. [蘇鑰機]. (2009). The influence of free newspapers on the market of Hong Kong readers [免費報紙對香港讀者市場的影響]. *Media Digest* [傳媒透視] 5, 6–8.

Tang, K. Y., Cheng, X., & So, Y. K. [鄧鍵一、程曉萱、蘇鑰機]. (2014). Newspapermen, news industry and Hong Kong social changes: Case studies of *Ming Pao, Hong Kong Economic Journal* and *Apple Daily* [報人、報業與香港社會變遷:《明報》、《信報》和《蘋果日報》的個案探討]. *Journal of International Communication* [國際新聞界], *36*(8), 23–37.

Trading Economics. (2017). Hong Kong Average Monthly Salaries 1999–2017. Retrieved from https://tradingeconomics.com/hong-kong/wages.

Tschang, F. T. (2009). Hong Kong's new creative industries. *Hong Kong Innovation Project: Report No. 11.* Retrieved from http://www.savantas.org/wp-content/uploads/2014/06/11_Tschang.pdf.

UK Department of Culture, Media and Sport. (1998). *Creative industries mapping document.* Retrieved from https://www.gov.uk/government/publications/creative-industries-mapping-documents-1998.

University of Hong Kong Centre for Cultural Policy Research. (2003). *Baseline study on Hong Kong's creative industries.* Retrieved from http://www.cpu.gov.hk/doc/en/research_reports/baseline study(eng).pdf.

Zuhdi, U. (2014) Analyzing the role of creative industries in the national economy of Japan: 1995–2005. *Open Journal of Applied Sciences, 4*, 197–211. Retrieved from http://dx.doi.org/10.4236/ojapps.2014.44020.

Chapter Three

The Game Industry and Market in China

THE GAME ECONOMY IN CHINA

China is perceived as a huge market for Hong Kong. Because China's game industry has grown tremendously over the past two decades, Hong Kong game companies would like to share in the benefits of this development. However, from a researcher's point of view, which is described in this chapter, the intention to develop the game industry in China is part of a national agenda. It has emerged as not only an economic force with transformative power in Chinese society but also as a means of promoting soft power overseas. Hence, China's companies should be more concerned than those in Hong Kong should with the so-called Asian rivalry. From the early development of China's game industry to 2010, Korean game companies took the lead because Chinese players were largely attracted to the localized Korean games (Chung & Fung, 2103). However, the discourse of East Asian rivalry drew the attention of Chinese officials and domestic players. As this chapter argues, China's domestic market players have assumed a leading position in the global market and have become a huge part of China's cultural economy. It is believed that in general, the game industry and other creative industries are dynamic and sustainable driving forces of the cultural economy, which is fast becoming the third-largest economic sector in Western cities and is playing an increasingly important role in East Asia (Hutton, 2015).

To understand the cultural economy, material practices—in this case, the game market and transactions—must be considered as both economic and cultural. These practices are regarded as "complex interferences" by the market, which are mandated by the state and official discourses (du Gay and Pryke, 2002, p. 22). With this dual interpretation in mind, in this chapter, I will focus on the formation and key elements of the game economy in China. In the following chapter, I will explain how the state interferes with, cultivates, or twists this cultural economy with a view to regaining market territory and expanding outward (to Asia and other countries) by means of implementing new cultural policies. Of course, the state's policy of protecting domestic market players is not the sole factor in the success of domestic market players and the industry at large. A huge domestic market, the strong cultural specificity of market demands, a sufficient talent pool, and a viable business model are key factors. Numerous studies have examined the factors that contribute to the economic miracle of China's game industry despite strong state control.

Some researchers have described the game economy as a leisure economy that is rooted in recreation, entertainment, and consumption rather than necessity (Xi, 2007). In addition, Li, Cui, and Han (2012) point out that online games are a form of e-commerce for profit. Driven by the Internet boom—as evident in increasing Internet penetration and the rising number of consumption activities on the Internet—the growth of the online game industry has overtaken that of other traditional industries as one of the fastest moving, up-and-coming economic sectors (Wu, 2000). In view of this tremendous potential for growth, previous studies have identified several key characteristics of the game industry in China.

Because the game industry is technology- and capital-intensive, developers are required to invest vast amounts of money in technological infrastructure—which carries high levels of business risk—before their products are launched. Nevertheless, the technology- and capital-intensive nature of the game industry also creates the advantage of economies of scale. Because a large proportion of investments are fixed capital and are spread over many units of output, the cost per unit decreases as business scale increases. The more copies that game companies produce, the lower the cost per game. Moreover, the game industry highly depends on user interaction. An online game becomes popular only if there is a considerable number of gamers playing it. It is unlikely that gamers will continue to play a game if only a few gamers are participating in it (Xue & Huang, 2006).

Coinciding with its rapidly growing economy, China's game industry has enjoyed tremendous growth in the past few years. According to Lu and Zhang (2012), the industry had grown rapidly and steadily since 2003. The total annual revenue was RMB¥2.57 billion in 2004, an increase of 45.8 percent. In 2007, the industry's total annual revenue reached RMB¥10.76 billion, an increase of 62.8 percent compared with the previous year. The annual revenue showed the greatest increase in 2008, with a growth of 72.5 percent. Statistics showed that China's total annual revenue reached RMB¥44.61 billion in 2011.

Despite this significant growth, China's online game industry has further potential. In 2010, China's online game industry accounted for only 4.8 percent of the global game industry's total market value (RMB¥728.6 billion), including arcade games, PC games, console games, online games, and mobile games, as well as one-third of the global online game industry's total market value (RMB¥99.3 billion). However, beginning in the first quarter of 2016, China's online game market surpassed that of the United States as the biggest online market in the world with a revenue of RMB¥41.5 billion (Statista, 2017). In 2017, the revenue increased to US$25.7 billion, accounting for one-quarter of the global revenue. A comparison of the game revenues of China, Japan, South Korea, and the United States is shown in table 3.1.

Thirty-Second Statistical Report on Internet Development in China reported that the number of online game users in China had increased from 335.69 million by the end of 2012 and had reached 345.33 million by the end of June 2013 (China Internet Network Information Center [CNNIC], 2013b). In this period, the number of mobile game users also increased. In August 2013, the number of mobile game users had reached 208 million, which accounted for 44.9 percent of mobile phone users (CNNIC, 2013a). The increase in the number of mobile game users occurred mainly because of China's high smartphone penetration, advanced mobile network, and changes in user behavior. Thus, despite the increase in the number of networked game users in general, the number of online game users decreased from 59.5 percent to 58.5 percent (CNNIC, 2013b). The latest data (CNNIC 2016) clearly show that the number of online game users has reached 391.48 million, or 56.9 percent of the total number of networked gamers. By comparison, in 2015, 45.1 percent of players used mobile games. Senior management of the game companies interviewed predicted that the market for mobile games would continue to grow and exceed that of online games.

The market segments of online games are also evolving rapidly. Prior to 2012, Internet-based client games were the most popular type of online

Table 3.1. Comparison of Game Revenue in 2017

Country	Game Revenue (in US$ Billion)
China	27.5
Japan	12.5
South Korea	4.2
United States	25.1
Global Total	*108.9*

Sources: Newzoo, 2017a, 2017b, 2017c.

games, accounting for 90 percent of market revenue from 2003 to 2008 and more than 80 percent of market revenue from 2009 to 2010. In 2010, the number of gamers in China had reached 215 million: 110 million gamers used MMORPG as well as online casual games; and 105 million gamers played web games (CNNIC, 2010). Social games, the most popular form of web game, had about 92.09 million users.

Although the growth of Internet-based client games has declined, casual games, web games, and mobile phone games are gaining in popularity. In 2011, Internet-based client games captured only 70 percent of market revenue (Lu & Zhang, 2012). In 2012, 53 percent of Chinese online games were Web games, followed by 23 percent client MMORPG, 18 percent client casual games, 4 percent social games, and 2 percent others. Other statistics showed that mobile games have emerged as an up-and-coming option for online gaming (Lu & Zhang, 2012).

Previous statistics showed that each market segment had different demographic characteristics. For example, of gamers who play MMORPG online casual games, 73.1 percent are male, 81.7 percent live in cities, 37.5 percent are aged between 20 and 29 years, 40.7 percent are students, and 50.4 percent are gamers with monthly incomes of less than RMB¥1,500 (CNNIC, 2011). Compared to the players of online chess games, the age groups were balanced: 28.2 percent were between 10 and 19 years, 31.6 percent were between 20 and 29 years, and 36.5 percent were 30 years or above. There was also a balance in terms of the gamers' professional backgrounds. The statistics showed that 29.8 percent were students, 19.1 percent were office workers, and 14.3 percent were freelance workers (Lu & Zhang, 2012). In other words, online chess games appealed to a wider audience compared to MMORPG or online casual games.

Mobile games have gradually become a part of their players' daily lives. For instance, 68.5 percent of gamers reported playing online games before they slept; 56.5 percent participated in online gaming on transportation and while waiting for a meeting; and 52.7 percent used it as a way to spend time during breaks at work or while waiting in line (CNNIC, 2013a). Statistics also showed that 65.2 percent of mobile games users participated in online gaming more than once a day, and over 80 percent spent more than thirty minutes online gaming every day (CNNIC, 2013a). Moreover, 84.0 percent of mobile game users played console games, and 45.8 percent played online games (CNNIC, 2013a).

The growth of the Chinese game empire is not accidental. Previous studies have shown that China's online game industry established a chain to support the massive scale of its domestic and overseas markets. The industrial chain in the game industry has two main kinds of links: "key links" and "supplementary links." Key links include developers, operators, channels, and users, who cooperate with each other but remain independent. Supplementary links are related industries such as IT, telecommunication, manufacturers of hardware and software, and publishing (Sun, 2007). The value created by key links in the industrial chain flows to the game industry, whereas the value created by supplementary links flows to related industries (Tang, 2004).

In China, the industrial chain in the game industry consists of four key links: developers, operators (or agents), distributors, and sales terminals. Developers and operators are the most important among the four (Hou, 2009). In fact, most operators can reach game users directly through network promotion and online payment, such as Alipay and e-banking. Hence distributors and sales terminals are less important than developers and operators.

Supplementary links include providers of Internet services, bandwidth, and equipment for game operators; PC manufacturers; server manufacturers; system safety manufacturers; and software platform manufacturers. For example, telecommunication and Internet servers provide the Internet and bandwidth used by operators; Internet data centers provide main engines and equipment; and Internet content providers manage the online promotion and sales of point cards.

The IT, telecommunication, and manufacturing industries are important supplementary links in the game industry. The development of the game industry has motivated the growth of manufacturers of PCs, which includes upgrading hardware and software and increasing bandwidth. These links also generate growth in related industries, such as toy and costume manufacturing.

In the most common model of revenue sharing between key industrial links and related industries in China, developers take 20 percent of the profit and operators take 50 percent, which includes 20 percent from customer service and 30 percent from value-added services. Different levels of agents, Internet cafes, and the media then take 30 percent of the profit. Hence it is important that an online game product create commercial benefits for both industrial links and related industries. According to the *2010 Annual Report on China's Online Game Market*, every 100 consumed by game users generated RMB¥92.5 of income in telecom broadband (including the cost of game users and operators), RMB¥83.9 in IT products, and RMB¥11.5 in channels (including channels of information, product, and disbursement; Ministry of Culture of the People's Republic of China, 2011). Another study indicates that every RMB¥1 million of revenue in the game industry generated as much as RMB¥15 million of revenue in related industries (Sun, 2007).

Because the game industry, similar to other creative industries in Asia, has become a large source of employment, particularly for young graduates, it is also seen as a way to solve the problem of youth unemployment. In China, despite its recent debut, the game industry nurtured 152 groups of game developers and employed as many as 36,660 professionals in 2012, 56 percent of whom were developers (19 percent of these were programmers, 20 percent were art designers, and 12 percent were planners) and 44 percent were non-developers (Ministry of Culture of the People's Republic of China, 2013).

The demographic profile of game professionals shows that their average age has increased. In 2007, 11 percent of the workforce in the game industry was below twenty years old, which is the average age of a high school graduate in China. In 2012, only 1 percent were younger than twenty. Coinciding with the educational background of players, the industry has attracted an increasing number of educated. According to a survey conducted in 2012, 7 percent of the industry workforce were high school or technical secondary school graduates, followed by 31 percent who were college graduates, 57 percent who held bachelor's degrees, and 5 percent who held master's or doctoral degrees (Ministry of Culture of the People's Republic of China, 2013).

The education level varied according to the role and the required competency of the individual. In general, the industry is easily accessible to candidates who have a wide range of education. For example, game planners require relatively little education. A twenty-year-old candidate with extensive gaming experience could join a game company even without a high school qualification. Most positions that require technical expertise, however, such as that of a programmer or software engineer, require at least a bachelor's degree. Because the game industry requires massive amount of graphic design, it has employed more art school graduates than other sectors have.

Because the game industry is also an emerging sector, industry professionals benefit from a relatively high level of monthly income. In 2012, 13 percent of the workforce was paid less than RMB¥3,500, compared with 65 percent of the workforce, who were paid RMB¥3,500–7,500 and 13 percent who were paid RMB¥10,000 or more. In Beijing, an average mainframe programmer was paid RMB¥10,000–15,000 per month, and a web developer was paid RMB¥10,000–20,000 (Ministry of Culture of the People's Republic of China, 2013). A development manager was paid between RMB¥20,000 and RMB¥30,000. This salary schedule does not take into account performance-based bonuses and other incentives. However, as I will explain in the next section, there is another side to the salary of a game professional or creative worker—in particular, the livelihoods of workers in this fast-changing industry can be unpredictable.

In China, the industrial chain of online games has nurtured many giant game companies, many of which are now big publicly listed corporations. The top ten game companies in China include Tencent Games (騰訊遊戲), NetEase Games (網易遊戲), Shanda Games (盛大遊戲), Changyou.com (搜狐暢遊), Perfect World (完美世界), Giant Interactive Group (巨人網絡),

GY Games (光宇華夏), Kingsoft (金山遊戲), Net Dragon Websoft (網龍), and TianCity (世紀天成). Most of these companies rely heavily on a few signature products to generate revenues of RMB¥20–30 million per year.

These companies are relatively recent, having been founded between 1995 and 2005. Established in 1995, Kingsoft is the oldest. Others, such as Shanda Games and Net Dragon Websoft, were established in 1999. NetEase Games (established in 2001), Changyou.com (established in 2002), Tencent Games (established in 2003), and Perfect World and Giant Interactive Group Inc. (established in 2004) are even more recent than Kingsoft, Shanda Games, and Net Dragon Websoft.

The top game companies in China play an increasingly important role in the online game industry. Report from Enfodesk at Analysys International identified a trend toward centralization in top game companies (Millward, 2012). In 2012, the top seven Chinese game companies accounted for 88.2 percent of the total game market revenue (RMB¥11.26 billion which is equivalent to US$1.78 billion) in China. Among these companies, the top three captured more than 67 percent of the revenue in China's game market. Tencent Games (騰訊遊戲) was the largest, and it contributed RMB¥3.76 billion (33.7 percent). NetEase Games (網易遊戲) and Shanda Games (盛大遊戲) ranked second and third, contributing RMB¥1.98 billion (17.3 percent) and RMB¥1.80 billion (16.0 percent), respectively (Millward, 2012). As the market grows, the giant companies' game market expand more and faster than that of smaller ones.

iResearch revealed that in 2012, the total revenue of Tencent Games grew to RMB¥23.11 billion—an increase of 37.0 percent. The total revenue of NetEase Games grew to RMB¥6.94 billion in 2012—an increase of 4.7 percent. Qihu 360 (奇虎360) and Kongzhong (空中網) joined the top ten companies in China's game industry in the same year (2013). This trend toward centralization has made it difficult for new game companies to compete. In 2016, the revenue of Tencent and NetEase was 59.3 percent of the entire online game market in China (Tang, 2016).

Of course, Chinese game companies are attracted to the global game market. Hence they have launched copyright businesses, cooperative operations, and independent operations. In 2007, China's game export volume was RMB¥0.34 billion, which grew to RMB¥2.2 billion in 2011, an increase of 57.2 percent (Lu & Zhang, 2012). In 2011 approximately one hundred Chinese game companies exported games to overseas markets according to the *2012 Annual Report on China's Online Game Market*, and the number of newly exported games was 66, of which 31 were web games, 17 were Internet-based client games, and 18 were mobile games (Ministry of Culture of the People's Republic of China, 2013). The most recent data shows that the export volume of Chinese games in 2012 was RMB¥3.49 billion, an increase of 57.5 percent and ten times that of 2007. The export volume increased by

177 games that were developed by forty Chinese game companies, including 63 Internet-based client games, 103 web games, and 11 mobile games (Chinanews, 2013).

The key markets for China's game exports are Hong Kong, Macau, Taiwan, Southeast Asia, Korea, and Japan. Other markets include Europe, North America, and South America. According to the *2012 Report on China's Online Game in Overseas Markets*, 113 games (26.7 percent) developed by Chinese companies were exported to Hong Kong, Macau, and Taiwan; 110 (26.0 percent) were exported to Southeast Asia; 79 (18.7 percent) were exported to Korea and Japan; 50 (11.8 percent) were exported to Europe; and the remaining (16.8 percent) were exported to North America, South America, and other areas (IDC, 2012).

The Taiwan market is of strategic importance to the game companies of mainland China. In 2012, 108 Mainland Chinese games (including Internet-based client games, web games, and mobile games) were exported to Taiwan. The market for Internet-based client games in Taiwan was dominated by Korean online games (39.7 percent), and mainland Chinese games only accounted for 8.6 percent. However, games developed by mainland Chinese companies dominated Taiwan's web games market.

Southeast Asia is another important market for mainland Chinese companies. In 2012, the total market revenue of Chinese games sold in Indonesia, Malaysia, the Philippines, Singapore, Thailand, and Vietnam exceeded RMB¥3.43 billion (IDC, 2012). Games developed by Chinese companies are very popular in Southeast Asia, where the market is less developed and has few game companies. Moreover, the cultural proximity of the Chinese populations in Southeast Asia and Mainland China has also contributed to the success of Chinese games in the Southeast Asian market.

Chinese game companies, however, do not have a large share of the European and North American market, partly because they face strong domestic competitors with first-class technology and products that are more culturally compatible with local audiences. A few Chinese game companies, Tencent Games for example, have acquired local game studios as a way to enter the European and North American market, but the room for Chinese companies marketing Chinese games is limited. First, while gamers in Europe and North America are used to 3D games, most games developed by Chinese companies are 2D or 2.5D. In terms of style, characters, and gameplay, Chinese games do not appeal to European and North American players. Second, because importers and distributers in Europe and North America share a sense of skepticism over Chinese games, Chinese game developers have to charge lower fees compared with Korean game developers.

Although Chinese web games appeal to a particular market segment in Japan and South Korea, the profits generated in these two markets are much lower than in Southeast Asia. There are several reasons to account for the low profit margin of Chinese games in these markets. First, because established domestic-market players dominate Internet-based client games and game machines, foreign companies, including Chinese game companies, have little room to compete. Second, domestic game operators in these countries tend to ask for a large share when it comes to profit sharing, which lowers the profits of Chinese companies.

Although Chinese game companies are expanding overseas, they do not rely heavily on overseas markets for profit, but cultural exports are definitely advocated by the Chinese government. Zhang Yunfan, chief executive officer of 178.com, one of the most popular game portals in China, has said there is no urgent need for Chinese companies to expand overseas because China's domestic market is big enough.

> Perfect World has already invested in the Japanese game market . . . The second generation of Chinese users employ Chinese servers (in China) to play Chinese online games. The U.S. online game market is not that prosperous . . . [though their] forms of entertainment are numerous, and the need for social networking is not as demanding [as in China]. The Chinese [in the United States] also use Chinese servers . . . . In the coming year, Tencent will gain at least 50 percent of the overseas market. (Interview May 16, 2010, in Beijing)

In other words, the giant game companies have already fulfilled the "mission" of expansion overseas. Moreover, to the question of whether there is a real need to continue this expansion, the probable answer is no, as the game companies in China already serve the needs of Chinese users overseas.

BUSINESS STRATEGIES AND SUSTAINABILITY

Most Chinese companies still focus on the Chinese market to sustain their business. This focus requires meticulous planning to devise strategies to cope with constant changes in the online game market, including market size, market segments, game exports, and industrial chains.

In China, most online games are based on one of three business models: charging by time, charging by item, or charging by deal. Charging by time refers to a business model in which users are charged for access to a game based on time. In most cases, gamers make a monthly payment for unlimited monthly access. Although this model does not generate huge profits, it cultivates a habit of paying for gaming in mainland China, where game piracy has been an issue. Charging by time used to be the most common model but it has been largely replaced by charging by item, introduced by Shanda Games in 2005. At first, the new business model led to a decrease in revenue, but it generated a remarkable market revenue of RMB¥0.31 billion in the first quarter of 2006. The idea of charging by item is "play for free, pay for items." Free participation is used as a hook to attract game users and cultivate a sense of loyalty to the game. On one hand, free participation encourages gamers to participate and thus expands the base of gamers in China. On the other hand, the amount of money that gamers spend buying items is much more than that spent in the charging-by-time monthly model because the player's expenses are not fixed. In general, most popular online games are now based on a charging-by-item model. Xu Xiao, who is in charge of the development department of NetEase Games, described the operation in China of the Korean dancing game *Audition Online*.

> Dating a girl [in the game] is easy. There are fewer girls than boys [and] they are willing to meet those [boys] who are rich and who are skillful in micro control [an online slang term meaning managing the skills in this context] . . . There is a system of marriage . . . Before marriage, [boys] have to purchase clothes and fashions for the girls. For example, in *Audition Online*, there are buttons on every piece of clothing. [A player] can purchase [a piece of clothing] or ask another player to purchase it [for them] . . . Boys also do the same. [A] high school [boy] might say, "I am cool. Buy me clothes." [Players] can create all sorts of relationships [in the game], including male-female relationships, family, blood-oath relationships, and parental relationships, and the only condition is money. (Interview April 13, 2010, in Beijing)

This explanation illustrates that in order to bond with players or simply enjoy the gameplay, to a certain degree gamers have to pay for items. The gameplay is so well designed that gamers are willing to pay for items in order to maximize their pleasure. On the business side, as I understood the developers' explanation, there are two structural reasons for the success of this business model. First, the "20-80 principle" (the assumption that only 20 percent of players look for games with sophistication and quality thus game developers target the remaining 80 percent) is similar to the social structure in China. That is, in China 10 percent of the population is upper class, 22 percent is middle class, and 68 percent is lower class (Lu, X., 2010). Hence, to maximize the game market, the game has to cater to the lower class, which is the majority. Making online games accessible and affordable to a large lower class then widens the pool of gamers. Free participation is the bait. Second, because most gamers are skeptical of newly developed games, free participation provides an opportunity for gamers to test a game before they actually spend their money on it.

Despite the proven success of charging by item, some game companies are experimenting with a new business model in which charges are by deal. This business model seeks to position online games as a platform of e-commerce, which allows transactions among users, the game company charging a commission for each transaction. *Lyv Se Zheng Tu* (綠色征途) is an example: gamers can trade items with other gamers, and the developer receives 5 percent of each transaction. Although this model is yet to become mainstream, it adds the dimension of e-commerce to online games.

The currently used business models pose challenges to key industrial links (Tang, 2004). First, because domestic game developers lack models of multiple profit generation, their products have low profitability. Second, most key players in the game industry are operators or agents of foreign imported games. Third, domestic operators lack autonomy, which limits the market development of derived products and constrains the establishment of comprehensive game communities, thus inhibiting the development of solidarity and loyalty among game users (Ren, 2004).

Online games are aimed at a mass market that has limited purchasing power. However, in-game advertising can further leverage and monetize the coverage of online games in the mass market. According to iResearch (2008), the revenue of online in-game advertising (IGA) reached US$1 billion in 2007, and it was expected to reach US$1.94 billion in 2011. IGA is now widely accepted as a major advertising outlet. In line with advertisers' perceptions, scholars believe that IGA is an effective way to advertise because people tend to remember brand names that appear in games (Yang, Roskos-Ewoldsen, Dinu, & Arpan, 2006). Because of the demographic profile of the majority of gamers, IGA is particularly popular in the fast-moving consumer goods industry.

Some advertising is common in online games. Product placement, commonly known as "sponsored items" (Fu & Lu, 2007), is frequent. For example, in *Freestyle*, the characters are designed to wear Nike sport shoes during their basketball games. Another example is *QQ Fantasy*. Characters in this game energize themselves by drinking Nutri-Express, a beverage produced by the food and beverage company Wahaha. Some developers even create advanced game items for particular sponsors. For instance, Joyzone, the game developer of *CT Racer*, collaborated with Faw-Volkswagen Automotive and placed a Volkswagen Sagitar in the game. "Stage setting" is another common form of advertising in online games. In this type of advertising, banners appear in the game's background. For instance, Nike, Adidas, and other sports brands advertise in sports games such as *FIFA* and *Need for Speed: Underground*.

Many popular online games that are sold across the globe tend to minimize their cultural origin; however, online games in China are culturally specific. This cultural specificity partly contributes to the success of Chinese online games in both domestic and overseas markets. For instance, MMORPG, the most popular type of online games in China, are based on Chinese folklore, legends, *wuxia*, and historical events. The cultural familiarity of online games not only appeals to gamers in domestic markets but also attracts the participation of overseas Chinese populations and gamers with an interest in Chinese culture. According to the data gathered in my interviews, in terms of key market exports, Southeast Asia was ranked highest, and it accounted for more than half of the market. It was then followed by Europe, North America, Japan, and South Korea. There is a considerable Chinese community throughout Southeast Asia in Malaysia, Thailand, Indonesia, and Vietnam. Malaysia alone has a Chinese population of 7 million.

Genghis Khan (2009) is a distinctive example of cultural specificity. Genghis Khan was founder and emperor of the Mongol Empire, which governed China from 1260 to 1370 as the Yuan Dynasty. Genghis Khan is widely considered the most powerful emperor in Chinese history. His territory included East Asia and Central Asia. The Beijing-based domestic online game company *Qilin Youxi* developed a series of online games based on this history. The games are in line with the ideal of "Chineseness," which focuses on a multicultural nation with strong military power. The series has been well received by the market, receiving numerous awards such as favorite online game in 2009. Previous studies have indicated that historical epic games such as *Genghis Khan* serve to foster national Chinese identity across the globe (Fung & Ho, 2016). However, this is not to say that Chinese game companies are intent on joining the state in producing hegemonic content for the sake of nationalism. In this case, cultural content coincides with market taste.

Other examples of this type of coincidence are *Journey to the West* and *Romance of the Three Kingdoms*, which are two novels that serve the same function of nationalism (Fung & Ho, 2016). *Journey to the West* features a Buddhist monk who seeks to explore his religion in the West during the Tang Dynasty. The text has been adapted for numerous online games, including *A Journey to the West*; *Pocketpet Journey West*; and a Q-version of *Journey to the West*. *Romance of the Three Kingdoms*, in turn, is a legend placed between the Han and Jin dynasties during the so-called Three Kingdoms era. The story has been incorporated into *Warriors of the 3 Kingdoms* (2011), *Chibi* (2007), *Yi San Guo* (2010), *QQ Three Kingdoms* (2012), *Map of the Three Kingdoms* (published annually from 2000 to 2013), and *Three Kingdoms Brawler* (2010).

Chinese game companies strengthen their business by producing games laden with strong references to Chinese culture. However, because of a relatively immature legal system, protecting their property from nonpaying access and use is an important task for game companies. *Waigua* are private, mainly illegal servers that operate independently of the game companies (Sun, 2007; Tang, 2004). According to MacInnes and Hu (2007), "*waigua* is a type of software designed to automatically conduct activities for players in order to quickly increase their level even when they are not actually at their computer" (p. 137). *Waigua* allows users to achieve high levels of game skill, experience, health, and wealth in a short period. According to a survey conducted by Sina in 2003, 51.8 percent of gamers (7.15 million gamers) reported that they had experience with *waigua* (Sun, 2007). While the percentage of *waigua* is increasing, the amount of time that users spend on gaming is decreasing. Thus, game company profits have decreased in recent years.

Private servers also harm the business of game developers and operators. MacInnes and Hu (2007) defined "private servers" as a situation in which "server source code is stolen, hacked or leaked" (p. 138). They also pointed out that "as a result some people set up their own game servers using the leaked source code" (p. 138). Because private servers charge lower fees, they significantly curtail the profit of game operators. According to a survey conducted by *Sina* in 2003, 30 percent of gamers (4.14 million) had had experiences with private servers (Sun, 2007), which implies that a large proportion of revenue is absorbed by the illegal operation of private servers.

But the data collected in the interviews revealed that the biggest challenge for small and medium-size game companies was not technical complexities or external threats, but a lack of talent. Despite the attractive remuneration packages they offer, game companies in China, in general, face a lack of human capital. First, in China, game companies are not perceived as employers of choice because the public sees games as addictive. Even though the industry has high business potential and offers room for career growth, it is still seen negatively by the public and the media because of this perceived effect on the young. For this reason, industry professionals do not enjoy the prestige enjoyed by their colleagues in other sectors, such as financial services and business consulting, even though their salaries are comparable. An interviewee who had previously worked as a senior game planner said that he had to move his career to journalism despite the lower salary because his parents were ashamed of his profession in the game industry. This stigma makes it difficult for game companies to retain talented employees, which results in the lack of a stable middle management. Even though experienced game workers stay with their company, in the interviews, they also expressed that working in the game industry was unstable. An experienced game programmer and his team left the game company Perfect World after they had developed *Three Kingdom Online*. This interviewee said that his team was well paid in the industry when there was a solid achievement. However, toward the end of the interview, he said, "[I] am now working in a big company; there is immense pressure. Now I am 26, feeling old, and can't afford to move to another company" (Interview July 18, 2010, in Beijing).

Furthermore, the industry lacks professional training programs in higher education. When the industry began, few universities offered relevant degree programs. Not until 2004 did universities establish programs related to game design, such as schools of animation and digital arts. And despite an increase in the number of courses and training programs, industry representatives in general doubt the quality of these programs. The chief technology officer of Beijing Rentianyou Internet Technology Company, which operates the major game platform 486g.com, summarized the problem:

> There is not enough [training] time for most of the fundamental courses [in universities]. There are 40 to 50 hours in one semester. If you work full time, guess how much time you have? Thus, one single database [in the game industry] needs a few semesters of study. Even though they graduate, they need another year of training [inside a game company]. To work in the game industry, at the very least, they have to learn how to operate two datasets, write Internet programming such as Linux, use DXDL game engines, game interfaces, and map editing devices (Interview June 13, 2010, in Beijing).

This interviewee implied that formal training in universities might not match the industry's expectations. Consequently, game companies have to offer their staff in-house training, such as seminars, forums, and mentorship programs, which creates additional business costs. Some large game companies, such as NetEase Games, Shanda Games, and Giant Interactive Group, recruit experienced game developers from small and medium-size game companies, which is their main strategy for acquiring talented employees. But this strategy significantly hurts the operation of those smaller companies because their developers may quit even before a product is completed.

THE CULTURAL MAGNET OF CHINA

The game industry has become a driving force in China's economy, from domestic market to exports. The industry's formula of cultural specificity appears to appeal to both local and overseas Chinese audiences. Because of the size of the Chinese population and the country's growing economy, the game industry has tremendous business potential here. Nevertheless, the game industry faces key challenges, such as illegal access to games and a lack of human capital, which hinders the industry from growing substantially and sustainably. The implications for China's emerging game industry and economy go beyond China's rising power and its potential soft power. China's game market has become a cultural magnet for Hong Kong game companies that aspire to cooperate with their counterparts on the mainland. Hong Kong has strong legal support, copyright protection, and talent development. However, China's business strategies and operations have developed without any connection to Hong Kong and its advantages.

My argument is that the burgeoning game and cultural economy in China, which are shaped by a multifarious mélange of government discourse, mandates, interventions, commercial motives, and technological factors, has been inflated perhaps initially in national discourse to a much bigger discourse and metanarrative (Wang, J., 2004). Jing Wang has long questioned the "place-specific economies of knowledge, creativity and production" (p. 9) and the feasibility of implanting a cultural economy and creative industries in Hong Kong based on China's experience, the socialist background of which, theoretically, is totally different from the capitalist history of Hong Kong. However, this discourse of cultural economy—supported by creative industries—is doubly infused in Hong Kong's public discourse. It is not about whether Hong Kong should make the creative industries an engine of GDP growth (which is a neutral argument) but whether Hong Kong can always take advantage of China's cultural economy. The concept of cultural economy is fluid, and the term *creative industries* could become an ideological buzzword. However, in reality, as we saw in chapter 2, the creative industries in Hong Kong have been surveyed by the government and framed as emergent industries, second only to the financial and service industries. But as I have suggested, the HKSAR tended to classify many industries—including some fringe sectors—as creative industries in order to project a promising picture of their collaboration with the Chinese market. The real issue is that Hong Kong is at a much later stage in fostering its creative industries compared to the rest of East Asia, including China. In fact, Hong Kong's cinema, Cantopop, TV dramas, and games are all precursors in the East Asian region. However, these market-driven enterprises have not been recognized as important assets of Hong Kong. Therefore, the government has not felt obliged to make a united, systematic, and conscious effort to promote and support these creative industries.

The aura of Hong Kong's creative industries has faded. Its game industry has been overshadowed by those of its East Asian neighbors in terms of volume and exports. Is it too late for the government to intervene and salvage the creative industries of Hong Kong? Is the discourse of this cultural economy practical or valid for Hong Kong? After Hong Kong was returned to China, the HKSAR became increasingly dependent on China's political economy. When this powerful discourse becomes hegemonic, will Hong Kong lose its autonomy? These critical questions are definitely unheard by the authorities. The answer, as I attempt to illustrate, lies in the models of Hong Kong's creative industries, cultural policy, and cultural economy that can and should be developed by taking advantage of the Chinese market while maintaining the autonomy guaranteed by "One Country, Two Systems."

Another scenario could be relevant. The assumption that China is a "back-up" market for Hong Kong is not defensible. If dependence on its motherland and Hong Kong's participation in the Chinese market be wishful thinking, how can Hong Kong retain the resources to stay abreast of other Asian competitors? As the following chapter on China's cultural policy will demonstrate, mainland China is concerned with developing its own strategy to cope with its Asian rivals in the gaming industry. Furthermore, among China's complex cultural policies for developing its cultural economy, there seems to be no place for Hong Kong.

Arjun Appadurai (1990) has long described a new global cultural economy, under which, in the names of global culture, one nation "cannibalizing" or conquering one another. Using Appadurai's words, I would argue that gaming and game industry can be seen as an example of "instrument of homogenization" in the politics of global culture. Today, China's cultural economy attracts not only Hong Kong companies and the companies of East Asia but global companies as well, including Disney, Universal Studios, and Hollywood, which all aspire to share in the fruit of this mushrooming market. However, a vigorous censorship system, unfavorable policies regarding overseas game companies, and financial support of local game companies in China which gives them a market and competitive advantage are evidence that it will not be easy for the companies of Hong Kong, East Asia, and other countries to share in China's cultural market. While the global media giants and transnational cultural corporations have high hope to conquer the China market, what they—deliberately or not—forget is that they have to face the challenge about being homogenized by China when they enter China. The strong discourse of the cultural economy of China also implies the prospect of global capital, but similar to the online game *King of Glory*, China has a high-level defense team that has surrounded itself with obstacles and minefields and has equipped itself with strong military power and currency. Thus, its challengers are not likely to win.

REFERENCES

Appadurai, A. (1990). Disjuncture and difference in the global cultural economy. *Media, Culture and Society*, 7(2): 295–310.
Bai, Y., & Gao, J. [白岩、高傑]. (2010). The discussion of establishment of online game stratification [淺析我國網絡遊戲分級制度的建立]. *Youth Journalist* [青年記者], *11*, 54.
Business Times. (2007). How to make a successful free online game [如何成功打造免費網游]. Retrieved from http://tech.qq.com/a/20070312/000122.htm.
Cao, Y., & Downing, J. D. H. (2008). The realities of virtual play: Video games and their industry in China. *Media, Culture & Society, 30*(4), 515–529.
Chinanews. (2013). 2012 Cultural exportation goes to two extremes, movie decreases 50 percent and game increases 50 percent [文化出口泰囧兩重天 電影減半遊戲增5成]. Retrieved from http://finance.chinanews.com/it/2013/02-22/4588362.shtml.
Chung, P., & Fung, A. (2013). Internet development and the commercialization of online gaming in China. In N. B. Huntemann & B. Aslinger (Eds.), *Gaming globally: Production, play and place* (pp. 233–250). New York: Palgrave.
China Internet Network Information Center (CNNIC) . (2010). *2010 report on online game users in China.*
CNNIC. (2011). *28th statistical report on Internet development in China.*
CNNIC. (2013a). *2013 report on entertainment activities of mobile phone users.*
CNNIC. (2013b). *32nd statistical report on Internet development in China.*
CNNIC. (2016). *37th statistical report on Internet development in China.*
Dang, J., & Liu, B. [黨婧、劉碧波]. (2013). The analysis of grey correlation of Chinese game industries and the related industries [我國網絡遊戲產業與關聯產業的灰色關聯度分析]. *Labor Security World* (theoretical edition) [勞動保障世界（理論版）], *2*, 98–101.

Du Gay, P., & Pryke, M. (2002). *Cultural economy: Cultural analysis and commercial life.* Thousand Oaks, CA: Sage Publications.

Ferguson, C. J. (2010). Video games and youth violence: A perspective analysis in adolescents. *Journal of Youth Adolescence, 40*(4), 377–391.

Fortier, D., & Fuller, G. (2006). *Debate: In-game advertisements.* Retrieved from http://www.mmorpg.com/showFeature.cfm/loadFeature/828.

Fu, X., & Lu, Q. [傅小龍，呂倩]. (2007). Research on advertising function and design pattern of network game [網絡遊戲中的廣告功效與設計模式探究]. *Packing Engineering* [包裝工程], *28*(2), 244–245.

Fung, A., & Ho, V. (2016). Cultural policy, Chinese national identity and globalization. In T. Flew, P. Iosifidis, & J. Steemers (Eds.), *Global media and national policies: The return of the state* (pp. 106–121). New York: Palgrave Macmillan.

Funk, M. (2007). I was a Chinese Internet addict: A tale of modern medicine. *Harper's*, pp. 65–73.

Gamelook. (2013). The list of top 20 online games in Internet cafés, League of Legends exceeds CF [網吧TOP20網游排行榜《英雄聯盟》超越CF]. Retrieved from http://news.duowan.com/1301/222778770035.html.

Golub, A., & Lingley, K. (2007). "Just like the Qing empire": Internet addiction, MMOGs, and moral crisis in contemporary China. *Games and Culture, 3*(1), 59–75.

Han, J., & Jia, S. (2003). The advertising potential of Chinese online games. *Journal of Zhejiang College of Politics and Law, 63*, 85–88.

韓冀，賈森橋. (2003). 〈國內網絡遊戲中的廣告商機〉。《杭州商學院學報》，第63期，頁85–88.

Hou, Y. [侯陽平]. (2009). *Analysis of local development strategies of Chinese online games* [中國網絡遊戲產業本土化發展策略探析]. (Unpublished master's thesis), Zhongnan University, Changsha.

Huang, W. [黃薇]. (2005). The fascination of online game advertisement [網絡遊戲廣告的魅力]. *Contemporary Communication* [當代傳播], *4*, 69–69.

Huang, Y. [黃盈]. (2008). The research and innovation of business models of Chinese online game operators [論中國網絡遊戲運營商盈利模式的研究和創新]. *Modern Business Trade Industry* [現代商貿工業], *5*, 314–315.

Huo, Y., Zhao, R., & Zhang, J. [霍煜梅、趙仁乾、張靜]. (2008). Moral evaluation model and its application in cyber games [網絡遊戲的道德評價模型及應用]. *Journal of Beijing University of Posts and Telecommunications (Social Science Edition)* [北京郵電大學學報], *10*(2), 29–31, 45.

Hutton, T. (2015). *Cities and the cultural economy.* London: Routledge.

IDC. (2012). *China gaming industry report.* Beijing: Renmin University Press.

iResearch. (2008). In-game advertising comes to stable development [遊戲內置廣告將步入平穩增長期]. Retrieved from http://a.iresearch.cn/fumeitiguanggao/20080218/76562.shtml.

Jiang, X [姜熙]. (2008). The analysis of structure of industrial chain of Chinese online game industries [我國網絡遊戲產業鏈結構分析]. *Science & Technology Association Forum* [科協論壇], *2*, 83.

Kelly, P. (2003). *In game advertising.* Retrieved from http://www.gamerseurope.com/articles/430/print.

Li, S., Cui, J., & Han, Y. [李升哲、崔基哲、韓勇]. (2012). Discussion of the business model of Chinese online game industries [我國網絡遊戲產業盈利模式的探討]. *Intelligence* [才智], *13*, 27–28.

Liu, Y. [劉依卿]. (2010). The thinking of in-game advertisement of online games: An analysis of Kaixin [網絡遊戲植入式廣告熱的冷思考——基於開心網的分析]. *Movie Review* [電影評介], *15*, 62–64.

Lu, B., & Zhang, Z. [盧斌、張璋]. (2012). Report on the development of China's Network Game Industry 2011 [2011中國網絡遊戲產業發展報告]. In B. Lu, Y. Zheng, & X. Niu [盧斌、鄭玉明、牛興偵]. (Eds.), *Annual report on development of China's animation industry (2012)* [中國動漫產業發展報告 (2012)]. (pp. 142–154). Beijing: Social Science Academic Press.

Lu, X. [陸學藝]. (Ed.). (2010). Social structure of contemporary China [當代中國社會結構]. Beijing: Social Science Academic Press.

Luo, R [駱容]. (2009). The characteristics of online games and their advertising models [從網絡遊戲的特殊性談廣告運營模式]. *News World* [新聞世界], *11*, 181–182.

Ma, X., & Liu, H. [馬小強、劉懷恩]. (2012). Discussion of online game stratification from the perspective of education [基於教育視角的網絡遊戲分級探析]. *E-Education Research* [電化教育研究], *234*, 69–73.

MacInnes, I., & Hu, L. (2007). Business models and operational issues in the Chinese online game industry. *Telematics and Informatics, 24*(2), 130–144.

Martinsons, M. G. (2005). Online games transform leisure time for young Chinese. *Communication of the ACM, 48*(4), 51.

Millward, S. (2012). Tencent's online gaming dominance grows as market expands to $1.78 billion. *TechinAsia.* Retrieved from https://www.techinasia.com/online-gaming-china-stats-2012-q1.

Ministry of Culture of the People's Republic of China. (2011) *2010 Annual Report on China's Online Game Market* [2010中国网络游戏市场年度报告]. Retrieved from http://miit.gov.cn/n1146290/n1146402/n1146455/c3226707/content.html.

Ministry of Culture of the People's Republic of China. (2013) *2012 Annual Report on China's Online Game Market* [2012中国网络游戏市场年度报告]. Retrieved from http://www.mcprc.gov.cn/whzx/bnsjdt/whscs/201304/t20130424_346054.html.

Newzoo. (2017a) The global game market will reach 108.9 billion in 2017 with mobile taking 42 percent. Retrieved from https://newzoo.com/insights/articles/the-global-games-market-will-reach-108-9-billion-in-2017-with-mobile-taking-42/.

Newzoo. (2017b). The Japanese gamer: Key consumer insights. Retrieved from https://newzoo.com/insights/infographics/the-japanese-gamer-2017/.

Newzoo. (2017c). South Korea. Retrieved from https://newzoo.com/insights/countries/south-korea/.

Pékin Zhihui Tour Information Technology Company. (2012). Imported online games enter China, domestic game industries are in the most difficult time during past 10 years [進口網游來勢洶洶　國產網游10年最難困境]. Retrieved from http://news.17173.com/content/2012-10-26/20121026103746765.shtml.

Qu, Q. [曲慶紅]. (2010). The analysis and influence of ethnics of online games [網絡遊戲倫理道德的分析和影響]. *Ming Ying Ke Ji* [民營科技], *5*, 151.

Ren, H. [任亨日]. (2004). Analysis of the industrial chain of network game and the business model [網絡遊戲產業鏈與商業模式分析]. *Shanghai Management Science* [上海管理科學], *1*, 53–54.

Shang, J., & Zhang, Z. [尚潔，張志遠]. (2010). Empirical analysis of the development of the Chinese online game industry [中國網絡遊戲產業發展實證分析]. *Consumer Guide* [消費導刊], *3*, 52–54.

Shang, Z., & Wang, S. [尚志紅、王素娟]. (2006). Legal thoughts on the classification of Internet games [網絡遊戲分級的法律思考]. *Journal of Guangxi Administrative Cadre Institute of Politics and Law* [廣西政法管理幹部學院學報], *21*(1), 41–45.

Shen, L. [申玲玲]. (2004). The pain and happiness of Chinese online games in 2004 [2004年的中國網絡遊戲痛并快樂著]. Retrieved from http://tech.sina.com.cn/other/2004-06-22/1640378850.shtml.

Statista. (2017). Revenues generated by online gaming in China from 1st quarter 2013 to 1st quarter 2016 (in billion yuan). Retrieved from https://www.statista.com/statistics/270112/revenues-of-china-online-gaming/.

Steinkuehler, C., & Williams, D. (2006). Where everybody knows your (screen) name: Online games as "third places." *Journal of Computer-Mediated Communication, 11*(4), 885–909.

Sun, J. [孫靖]. (2007). A study of the development and management of the online game industry [網絡遊戲產業的發展與管理研究]. *Tongji University Journal (Social Science Section)* [同濟大學學報（社會科學版）], *18*(1), 101–106.

Tang, I. (2016, August 9) Tencent-NetEase take 70 percent of Chinese mobile game market. Retrieved from https://seekingalpha.com/article/4002797-tencent-netease-take-70-percent-chinese-mobile-games-market .

Tang, L. [唐磊]. (2004). The grey industrial chain of Chinese online games [中國網游的灰色產業鏈]. *IT Time Week ly* [IT時代周刊], *1*, 18–19.

Wang, J. (2004). The global reach of a new discourse: How far can "creative industries" travel? *International Journal of Cultural Studies, 7*(1), 9–19.

Wang, J., & Cheng, H. [王靜，程浩]. (2008). Exploration of the Internet game advertisement's value and format [試析網絡遊戲廣告的價值與形式]. *Advertising Panorama* [廣告大觀（理論版)], *1*, 22–26.

Wang, L. [王麗娟]. (2008). Forms and features of advertisements in cyber games [淺談網絡遊戲廣告的形式與特點]. *Art and Design* [藝術與設計（理論)], *2*, 74–75.

Wang, Y. J. (2003). The market environment of online games needs regulations. Retrieved from http://www.pcgames.com.cn/netgames/netbbs/0311/240997.html.

Wu, J. [烏家培]. (2000). The Internet economy and its influence on economic theories [網絡經濟及其對經濟理論的影響]. *Academic Research* [学术研究], *1*, 5–11.

Xi, S. [奚聲慧]. (2007). *An economic analysis of the online game industry* [網絡遊戲產業之經濟學分析]. (Unpublished doctoral dissertation). Shanghai Academy of Social Science, Shanghai.

Xue, Ming., & Huang, J. [薛明、黃娟娟]. (2006). An industrial economics analysis of online games [網絡遊戲的產業經濟學分析]. *Technology Information* [科技資], *31*, 182–183.

Yang, J., & Guo, J. [楊健、郭建中]. (2004). On the Chinese Internet game industry [試論中國的網絡遊戲產業]. *Journal of Shanghai University (Social Science)* [上海大學學報（社會科學版)], *11*(1), 85–90.

Yang, M., Roskos-Ewolden, D. R., Dinu, L., & Arpan, L. M. (2006). The effectiveness of "in-game advertising": Comparing college students' explicit and implicit memory for brand names. *Journal of Advertising, 55*(4), 143–152.

Ye, H. [葉慧娟]. (2011). Comparative research on game rating systems [網絡遊戲分級制度比較研究] *Journal of East China University of Science and Technology (Social Science Edition)* [華東理工大學學報（社會科學版)], *2*, 83–90, 116.

Zhang, C., & Ma, L. [張晨、馬良]. (2004). Stratification of online games: Is it necessary? [網游分級：必須還是多餘？]. *Science Technology for China's Mass Media* [中國傳媒科技], *12*, 37–39.

Chapter Four

Cultural Policies in China

APPROACHES TO CULTURAL POLICIES

This chapter examines China's cultural policies vis-à-vis computer gaming. Because of a general embargo on gaming devices from outside the country, the first console video game in China was not developed until the 1980s (Fung & Liao, 2015). How did China evolve into the largest game market in the world in the past thirty years? It has been demonstrated that China's state policy supports the production of games domestically, fast tracks their development, and incentivizes their export. Thus China's market for games and its rapid expansion were formulated by the state's cultural policy. Before examining this cultural policy, it is worth understanding its nature in the Chinese context, particularly the ways in which games and gaming have become a part of Chinese culture that is legitimized and supported by the authorities.

The fact that culture is a highly contested concept (Gray, 2009) implies that the concept of cultural policies has multiple definitions and that there is no single approach to examining cultural policy (Gray, 1996). Studies related to cultural policies have been conducted in the fields of media and communications, cultural studies, cultural geography sociology, and political science. Such research has also been conducted in practical fields such as management, urban planning, and economics. In many instances, academics have adopted vastly different paradigms, approaches, and analytical tools to examine cultural policies. I have discussed the approaches of some cultural theorists who either consider the cautious interactions among culture, politics, creativity, and labor (Hesmondhalgh, 2012) or ascribe precarity to certain cultural industries (Rossiter, 2016). In this chapter, I would like to introduce a pragmatic approach to the investigation of cultural industries. From the point of view of an urban planner or an economist, a fundamental assumption in cultural policy making is that culture can be planned according to models of thinking, which eventually lead to various social benefits, such as employment and economic growth (Evans, 2001). In this macro sense, culture and cultural production are considered to belong to the private realm. From the perspective of public policy, the management of culture, specifically in the gaming industry, is part of a state's cultural estate (Craik, 2007). Historically, the management and planning of culture in Europe (Evans, 2001) and Asia (Fung & Erni, 2013) demonstrate the need for a cultural policy regarding the development of the game industry in Hong Kong.

Contrary to the approach taken by urban planners and economists, cultural studies tend to treat culture, cultural policies, and other recorded experiences as texts to be decoded and interpreted critically (McGuigan & Gilmore, 2002). Therefore, cultural policy has become a series of texts that are subject to the interpretations of the individual analyst rather than a set of concrete, organizational practices to be analyzed, even if the latter are addressed in the policy shifts that cultural studies originally intended to address (Bennett, 1996, pp. 307–308). While such intellectual readings of cultural policy bring to light the ideological control and hegemonic interests of otherwise taken-for-granted policies, they also run the risk of failing to generate relevant policy recommendations for concrete actions to be taken by the agents concerned. Hence, recent scholarship (e.g., Ahearne & Bennett, 2013) has reminded us that while the concerns of intellectuals and policy makers may be polarized, cultural studies require an approach that defines and analyzes cultural policies that are aimed at generating policy recommendation packages that consider the cultural values of public life. Moreover, in framing culture as an industry, a relationship between culture and social and economic realities is acknowledged (Bashford & Langley, 2000).

Economists approach cultural policy studies by analyzing a government's application of particular economic concepts and theories to resolve issues of cultural production and cultural management (Towse, 2014). In some cases, the state's intervention in the economy of cultural trade and flow, which overrides vested and other interests, can lead to a much healthier development of the cultural industry (O'Hagan, 1998). Certain economists (Frey, 2013) would even suggest integrating cultural policy into economics, or vice versa. In this respect, the focus is on concrete economic policies, such as taxation and direct public support, that governments create, utilize, and promote for cultural purposes within the cultural arena instead of on the cultural content of such policies. The emerging topics discussed in the East Asian cases considered in this chapter, such as cultural labor, copyright issues, and cultural economy are also of concern (Towse, 2014). In the game industry, this approach can be interpreted as employing economic policies to promote broader cultural development. This chapter will also investigate how other policy areas (e.g. educational policy and regulatory legal policies) affect cultural production or culture in general. In the last two sections of this chapter, the cultural policy of China is analyzed based mainly on this perspective in addition to elements of cultural studies and views of political scientists.

Political scientists regard cultural policy as both state action and state inaction in the cultural arena. The assumption is that the range of actions that governments take shed light on the prevailing values and ideology that they endorse. A major drawback is that such analyses often define cultural policy as "whatever it is that governments say it is, leading to a range of country-specific sets of actions, organizations and choices as the focus of study" (Gray, 1996, pp. 214–215). As I discussed in chapter 3, in the case of China's cultural policy, the national government of China has defined the range of creative industries to be supported and the limit of the actions to be taken, which then trickles down to all provincial, municipal, and city levels. In addition, the ideological control, censorship, and effectiveness of specific strategies appear to be gauged only in terms of the quantity of cultural products produced; the quality of the products is not questioned. Regarding this aspect, the culturalist approach reminds us that governmental agendas should not dominate and rationalize culture and policy and that cultural development, diversity, civic society, and inequality are also important considerations in the process (McGuigan, 2004). Sociologists and anthropologists have added other dimensions to cultural policy by studying the roles of both individuals and communities and ultimately addressing the discourse of power and subjectivity that often remains invisible in political approaches (Shore & Wright, 2003).

CHINA'S CULTURAL POLICIES

The game industry in China is seen as a both a model and market for Hong Kong. However, in China, emerging markets and models are not the result of a laissez-faire policy. To the contrary, they are driven by cultural policies on different levels, national, provincial, and municipal. Cultural policies, in addition to a rising GDP and a population of 1.4 billion, are viewed as a primary factor in China's success. Based on my own judgment, in terms of the type of support of the game industry, I would say that China's model is modeled on Korea's comprehensive cultural policy. On one hand, because Hong Kong is a special region of China, there is a continuous discourse about taking advantage of such policies to share the revenues of the market, although in practice, the results are mixed. On the other hand, through CreateHK, Hong Kong attempts to mimic cultural policies in China, which are far more extreme than in any other Asian country.

Similar to other industries, cultural industries, including the game industry, are seen as contributing to the economic development of contemporary
China. Moreover, cultural industries are always touted as drivers of innovation in China. Of course, when these industries contribute economic value
and produce "appropriate" content, they are viewed as conducive to social
stability and harmony, which is a political necessity in China. Hence, because of the importance of the cultural industries, the Chinese government
invests a large amount of resources in them, revises the overall blueprint for
their development every five years, and releases specific policies aimed at
different sectors of these industries.

The Chinese government creates guidelines for policies every five years.
The guidelines are called "Five-Year Plans" and comprise a series of social
and economic development initiatives. The purpose of these plans is to establish principles for the development of China by mapping strategies, setting
growth targets, and launching reforms. Since the 10th Five-Year Plan in
2002, cultural industries have been singled out by the Chinese government.
The Five-Year Plans in the most recent decade and the guidelines of cultural
policies in China are examined in this section.

In 2002, the Chinese government provided an official definition of cultural industries in the 10th Five-Year Plan, further distinguishing core, peripheral, and culture-related industries. According to the plan, the major cultural
industries include the visual arts, crafts, the performing arts, heritage, film
and video (including cartoons and animation), television and radio, online
games and new media, music, publishing, fashion, design, architecture, and
advertising (Kern, Smits, & Wang, 2011, p. 10). In 2002, regarding the
guiding ideology "Three Represents," former general secretary Jiang Zemin
stated that the Communist Party of China should strategize to produce policies that promote the advancement of productive social forces, culture, and
the fundamental interests of the majority of the people in China. The major
guideline of the 10th Five-Year Plan was the continuation of socialism in
China. At the industrial level, policies cater to adjusting and optimizing the
structure of cultural industries with priority given to social benefit. Reform is
the driver of the development of the cultural industries by remaining market-
oriented, enhancing the ability of self-administration within these industries,
and encouraging intellectual, technological, administrative, and systemic innovation. The 10th Five-Year Plan set targets for the development of specific
industries, including the performing arts, film and video, music, tourism, and
crafts. It included policies for financial support, tax incentives, and talent
training (National People's Congress, 2001).

This plan was followed by the 11th Five-Year Plan, which laid down a
blueprint for development from 2006 to 2010. In the 11th Five-Year Plan, the
reform of the cultural system was a key point. In order to improve the
cultural market, the government should implement policies on cultural indus-

tries, develop and regulate the participation of private capital in cultural industries, and adopt favorable elements of foreign culture. The 11th Five-Year Plan also encouraged the rapid development of new media and international cultural communication. It indicated that the state should develop digital broadcasting media, the digital publishing industry, and the online media industry. It also emphasized the importance of international cultural communication, the development of international cultural markets, and the promotion of Chinese culture to the world (National People's Congress, 2006).

In 2012, the Central Propaganda Department published a document outlining China's cultural policies for the next five years. There were some new points, but no radical changes. The most interesting point was that the spirit of a harmonious society was emphasized throughout the document, including sincerity and honesty in government, business, and society. The document also emphasized the important role of history and Chinese characteristics. In line with the 11th Five-Year Plan, an international tendency to media policy was reiterated in the 2012 document. The document stated that China should employ international organizations to promote its cultural agenda at the global level. It also advocated engagement with neighboring countries and other countries to enhance China's cultural policies (National People's Congress, 2011).

I argue that this document introduced the innovation concept of cultural governance, which was not considered in previous plans, based on the assumption that culture was a form of propaganda. Cultural governance means that it is legitimate for the Chinese central government to intervene in developing cultural activities for the sake of the nation. The Chinese cultural governance model is strongly centralized, and the major political and legislative powers involved are administered at the national level. The national government controls the cultural industries through different administrative bodies. All cultural activities, such as the import and export of cultural works and licenses for publication or distribution, must be approved by ministries in the national government.

The most important administrative body in this respect, the Ministry of Culture (MOC), deals with general cultural activities and is in charge of making regulations and granting licenses to all cultural activities. Within the MOC, different departments and bureaus are in charge of varied sectors of the cultural industries. The State Administration of Radio, Film, and TV (SARFT) includes the roles of policy planner, legislator, and supervisor in the audiovisual field, whereas the General Administration of Press and Publication (GAPP) regulates and censors publications. These two bureaus work in tandem, although they sometimes conflict in terms of jurisdiction, to draft laws and regulations and to regulate broadcasting, press, and publication activities. They also censor the content of TV, radio programs, and publications as a means of ideological control. SARFT regulates China National

Radio, China Radio International, and China Central Television. GAPP manages the state-owned publishing companies and approves publication licenses for periodicals, books, and music (Kern et al., 2011, p. 30). Since 2013, the function of SARFT and GAPP has been combined under the State Administration of Press, Publication, Radio, Film and Television (SAPPRFT).

The Department of Cultural Market Administration (DCMA) is in charge of making regulations for cultural markets and cultural products. The Bureau for External Cultural Relations (BECR) deals with foreign affairs in cultural works, and it is also responsible for handling cultural communication between China and foreign countries. Because the cultural industries have been assigned greater importance than previously, the Department of Cultural Industry (DCI) was established in 2006 (Kern et al., 2011) to engage in research and design plans, policies, and regulations for different sectors of the cultural industries.

Although the regulation of the cultural industries is highly centralized, regional and municipal governments are increasingly interested in extending their influence in this area because they have realized the potential social and economic benefits of developing these industries. Thus they have begun to collaborate with the central authorities in adopting regional and municipal cultural strategies and policies to develop the cultural industries in their own regions.

The 11th Five-Year Plan stated that China should "satisfy the increasing demand of the people for better cultural and spiritual life" with the ultimate goal of building a harmonious society (National People's Congress, 2006). In order to realize this mission, the Chinese government implemented two sets of cultural policy agendas. In one set, the Chinese government aims at developing the domestic cultural market and the cultural industries. *Report at the 17th National Congress of the CPC* (Hu, 2007) and *Report of the Work of the Government of 2009* (Xinhua News Agency, 2009a) stated that the People's Republic of China (PRC) aims at "adapting the cultural and creative industries to the specificities of the domestic market and to the specific 'local culture.'" Another specific work program described in the document is the utilization of "banking sector investment to promote the cultural industries." In order to reinforce Chinese domestic brands and cultural industries, foreign shareholders and direct foreign investment would be welcomed, which is the reason that Korean game companies were not prevented from entering the Chinese market. However, foreign shareholders and investments would be expected to fulfill "China's particular characteristics," which means that they could not contradict the PRC's ideology.

The second set of agendas concerned the attractiveness of the global market for the creative industries. In 2017, the global revenues of creative industries reached US$2,250 billion (World Creative, 2017). China was now willing to become a global leader of the creative industries. The document included an agenda for a "go global strategy" for China's cultural industries. According to this agenda, China would focus on the international scene and enhance its international cultural impact through the creation of platforms for cooperation. China would export cultural products that would be perceived as "Created in China," not "Made in China" (see Keane, 2007). Hence, the second set of agendas was aimed at enhancing the cultural influence of China, thus increasing its soft power. However, this could be wishful thinking on the part of the authorities because the last major success of a cultural export was probably Zhang Yimou's *Hero* (2002), which was fifteen years ago.

However, because of the push by the centralized authorities, the major cities in China also set their own agendas for cultural policies. Beijing, Shanghai, and Shenzhen established strategies to develop their cultural industries, and they have become leading hubs of creative culture in China.

Beijing aims to promote the creative industries by strengthening organizational coordination and established relevant guidelines and preferential policies. Shanghai has already included cultural and creative industries in its current plan, and it is willing to add further elements to enhance their competitiveness. Shenzhen, a new city, is an emerging center of creative culture in South China. The key cultural industries in Shenzhen are media, animation and games, publishing and circulation, creative design, printing, TV, films and videos, the performing arts, and leisure tourism (Kern et al., 2011). Instead of focusing on ancient culture and cultural history as do Beijing and Shanghai, Shenzhen aims to develop as a "famous modern city of culture."

Under the guidance of such documents, administrative bodies at national, regional, and municipal levels establish specific programs to promote cultural industries. These policies have led to the rapid development of the cultural industries in China during the past ten years. Among all sectors of the cultural industries, online games and new media are the fastest-growing creative sectors. In addition to these sectors, traditional media such as television, radio, and the publishing industries are strong. The film and video sector is on the rise. Moreover, design and architecture are important in China because they not only make a huge contribution to the Chinese economy but also reflect the shift from "Made in China" to "Created in China." Music and the performing arts are weak, but they benefit from the market and changes in the system. The visual arts and cultural heritage attract investors and tourists, and they convey positive images of China to the rest of the world (Kern et al., 2011).

In sum, China's cultural governance holds culture as a guiding ideology. Every five years, a plan is devised to guide the development of the cultural industries, and in this process, the central government has political and legislative power over cultural industries and activities. The agendas that guide

China's cultural policies include both developing the domestic cultural market and increasing its ability to compete globally.

In the 1990s, the development of the cultural industries was emphasized as a core issue in *The Central Committee of the Communist Party of China's Recommendation of the Ninth Five-Year Plan for National Economic and Social Development* (Central Committee of the Communist Party of China, 1995). This recommendation included the statement that "China should keep carrying out policies of supporting the development of cultural industries." In 1996, the State Council released *Provision of the State Council for Further Making Perfect Economic Policy on Culture* and stated that cultural industries were supported by national financial policies and tax policies (China-lawinfo, 2017a). In *Plan on Reinvigoration of the Cultural Industry*, released in 2009, gaming, which referred only to computer and online games in this specific context, was listed as one of the major sectors of cultural creation that was enthusiastically supported by the PRC. The authorities also expected to enhance the influence of the game industry "to help fuel the boom of the relevant service sector and manufacturing sector" (General Office of the State Council, 2009). As one of the important sectors of Internet service industry, the game industry emerged with the development of the Internet, and its operation has been integrated with communication services. The Chinese government established a series of policies and several general regulations of the game industry.

At this point, I have to note that such game policies are manifold. In presenting some details of these government policies in this chapter, my main argument is that the government uses political means to intervene in the game market, which has resulted in the blossoming of the game industry and the increased export of games produced in China. However, that does not mean that private capital is not invested in this market. My argument is that the prosperity of the game market is due to market demand, but because the government has promoted this market, it has expanded rapidly in China. Nevertheless, although some game products might not be commercially viable, they do serve ideological purposes.

Such political control as market control is mainly exercised by the MOC and the Ministry of Information Industry (MII). *Some Opinion of the Ministry of Culture and the Ministry of Information Industry on the Development and Administration of Net Games*, which was released by the MOC and MII in December 2005, presented the philosophy of China's development and administration of the game industry. First, this document described the current situation of the game industry in China, indicating that the industry remained "in the early stage of development with many problems that cannot be ignored." The most prominent problem was the illegal or immoral content of games. It was also very problematic that "game products with self-owned intellectual property right[s] cannot take the lead in the market." "Duplicated operational modes and monotonous product types" were the main impediments of the developing game industry. Further, "private server" and "game upgrade software download[s]" (*waigua*) damaged the market order. Serious social problems were also thought to be created by online gaming.

Regarding the current situation of the game industry, the MOC and MII have precise objectives of development that include building an industrial support system, implementing a project for fine-motor-skills games, fostering the game industry, and developing industries related to online games. The PRC aims at developing the industrial value of the game industry as well as building a healthy online cultural environment for minors. The Chinese government also encourages domestic game producers to enter the international market at the proper time, which is an indicator of the increasing international influence of Chinese culture.

In this document, the MOC and MII announced principles of regulating the market order of online games. The document states that the Chinese government "should be rigorous with the market access and intensify the supervision and control of the content"; "intensify the administration of the import of net game products"; "intensify the crack-down on such irregularities as 'private server' or 'game upgrade software download[s]'"; "effectively intensify the administration of net bars and regulate the market order of net bars"; and "intensify the industrial self-discipline and social supervision" (Ministry of Culture & Ministry of Information Industry, 2005).

In China, most popular games are imported from Korea, Japan, and the United States. In an interview, Liu Yusu (劉兩愫), vice dean of the Animation and Game Research Center of the Institute for Cultural Industries at Peking University, revealed that the market share of dozens of imported online games was about 40 percent, while the market share of hundreds of domestic online games was about 60 percent in 2009 (Interview July 20, 2010, in Beijing).

In order to protect the domestic game industry, the Chinese government announced policies to control the volume and the content of imported online games. *Notice of the General Administration of Press and Publication of Strengthening the Administration of Examination and Approval of Imported Online Games* stated that the General Administration of Press and Publication (GAPP) would be responsible for "conducting pre-approval on the online publication and issuance of game publications. Any enterprise engaging in the publication and operation service of online games within the territory of China shall be subject to the pre-approval of the GAPP, and obtain the license of providing publication service on the Internet with online game publication included in the service scope." That is, the GAPP is the one and only department that is authorized by the State Council, and all imported online games need its approval before they enter the Chinese market (General Administration of Press and Publication, 2009).

Three months after the release of this document, the China Copyright Office (CCO) and the GAPP enacted another policy and further elaborated the administration of the examination and approval of imported online games. This document clearly defined "imported online games" as "Internet game works authorized by overseas copyright owners." It also stated that the GAPP is responsible for the examination and approval of imported online games. No entity or individual would be allowed to engage in the operations and services of online games without the approval of the GAPP (China Copyright Office & General Administration of Press and Publication [CCO & GAPP], 2009).

According to *Interim Measures for the Administration of Online Games*, which was released by the MOC in 2010, examination of imported games and content censorship is necessary. The examination committee is constituted of scholars from different disciplines. The poll includes thirty to fifty experts and committee members, which change every two years. The experts are from education, sociology, economics, film studies, psychology, and relevant disciplines. According to Liu Yusu, a committee member, someone extracts the main content of online games to be examined and presents it to the experts (Interview with Liu Yusu, July 20, 2010, in Beijing). Violent, pornographic, and reactionary content in imported online games is censored. Content that is unacceptable must be returned to the company for revision and resubmission. For example, a tomb appears when a character resuscitates in *World of Warcraft*, and this was regarded as inappropriate content by the censorship committee (Interview with Liu Yusu, July 20, 2010, in Beijing). The tomb in this context represents a folklore superstition that implies the presence of a spirit in reality, which is in stark contrast to the communist ideology. I would like to emphasize here that the banning of superstition, spirits, and ghosts—as well as religious beliefs—is a universal Chinese cultural content requirement, especially in films and television dramas. However, the censorship of such immaterial forms is not particularly stringent in games.

An example of Chinese game censorship is *Battlefield 4*, which the MOC prevented from circulating in China at the end of December 2013. Developed by the Swedish video game developer EA Digital Illusions CE, *Battlefield 4* is one of the most popular games in the world. The sales volume of *Battlefield 4* reached US$6 million two months after its release. However, the MOC declared that it was an illegal online game and censored all information about it within China. The reason was that the game context depicted is a hypothetical Chinese civil war in 2020 in which Admiral Chang, the main antagonist, planned to overthrow China's current government. If he succeeded, Chang would have the full support of the Russians, bringing China to the brink of war with the United States. A commentary in *China National Defense News* indicated clearly that repeated exposure to such games might cause game players to develop the false impression that China is an unstable nation seething with political unrest and that the Chinese People's Liberation Army was an aggressive force. This game was regarded as a vehicle for the promulgation of American values. It was considered malicious slander and a cultural invasion of China. Because of this, the downloading or circulation of this game in China was forbidden (Liu, 2014).

In addition to formal examination of the contents of imported online games, the Chinese government strictly restrains the operations and services of foreign investors. In *Notice of the General Administration of Press and Publication, the National Copyright Administration and the Office of the National Work Group for "Combating Pornography and Illegal Publications" on Implementing the Provisions of the State Council on "Three Determinations" and the Relevant Explanations of the State Commission Office for Public Sector Reform and Further Strengthening the Administration of the Pre-approval of Online Games and Examination and Approval of Imported Online Games*, it is emphasized that "foreign investors shall be prohibited from investing in the operations and services of online games within the People's Republic of China in the forms of sole proprietorship, equity or contractual joint venture" (CCO & GAPP, 2009).

However, it is fair to say that the PRC's attitude toward the game industry is quite different from its attitude toward other creative industries. For example, the identification of any undesirable content in a film can lead to a total ban, whereas the content of animation is regulated only for users eighteen and under (Fung, 2016). With regard to the game industry, the classification of online games was initiated by the semiofficial agency China Youth Association for Network Development in 2004.

A program titled Green Games Recommendable Regulation was initiated to encourage self-regulation of the Internet sector. It defined games that were suitable for players younger than eighteen. The program uses five static indicators and seven dynamic indicators. The static indicators are degree of violence, degree of pornography, degree of horror, degree of social morality, and degree of cultural connotation. The dynamic indicators include player kill (PK) actions, illegal software, civilization of chatting systems, social order within games, game promotion, time-limit gaming, and social responsibility. Based on these twelve indicators, online games are categorized using five levels: General; Junior Middle School Student+; High School Student+; 18+; and Dangerous. Games in the General category are suitable for all ages, including minors, and the degree of violence in these games is minimal. Games in the Dangerous category contain "malignant" events (Song & Zhang, 2004), and they are banned. Games that are suitable for players under eighteen years old are considered "green games" (Fang, 2004; Tang, 2004).

In 2010, scholars at the Institute for Cultural Industries, Peking University, finished another classification of online games. This classification uses five indicators: cultural value, sensory comfort, time limit, antagonism, and health of the virtual society. The indicators are used to evaluate the content, basic structure, incidental music, and settings of games (Interview with Liu Yusu, July 20, 2010, in Beijing). Online games are then assigned one of three levels: General; 12 to 18 Years; or 18+ Years. Using this classification method, the scholars classified *FIFA Online* as General, meaning it was suitable for all players. *Zheng Tu* (征途) was classified as 18+ Years, meaning it was not suitable for players younger than eighteen (YXdown.com, 2017). Scholars at Peking University argued that this classification scheme was better than the then-current system. Also, the classification system favored the expanding game market in China. Xiang Yong (向勇), vice director of the Institute for Cultural Industries of Peking University, believed that the initial classification system was fundamentally flawed: it oversimplified the games as either good or bad, and this in turn was detrimental to the development of the game industry. In contrast, the second classification system was designed for a specific market and therefore it promoted the game industry (People.cn, 2010). Online games are interactive, and the players influence each other in the games. Thus Liu Yusu argues in this case that it is necessary to establish a classification system designed specifically for online games rather than simply adopt a movie-rating-type system (Interview July 20, 2010, in Beijing).

However, this attempt to establish a classification system for online games has not yet been recognized by officials. The vice director of the Culture Market Department of the MOC announced that the age-rating system "would not be built" due to the complexity of the game market (Zhang, 2010). According to a media report, MOC officials stated that this classification scheme for online games was the research product of certain academic institutions rather than a work project of the MOC. Moreover, the MOC was going to strengthen the administration of online games instead of borrowing a classification system from foreign countries (17173.com, 2017). At present, the designated administrative bodies regulate and administer the game industry, and game scholars continue to discuss the possibility of establishing a classification system in the future. In reality, because a purely administrative body censors game content, the state benefits because a large number of games from other countries are prevented from entering the Chinese market. In this way, the state has an opportunity to boost the competitive power of China's industries.

In 2008, the State Council released *Opinions of the General Office of the State Council on Implementing Some Policies and Measures for Accelerating the Development of the Service Sector*, which proposed a series of policies for promoting the development of service industries, especially modern service industries such as software and information. The game industry, which is a growing electronic service industry, was highly encouraged by the policies described in this directive (General Office of the State Council, 2008).

First, the policies indicated that public financial support of the development of the service sector should increase. According to the directive, "the special fund and the guidance fund for development of the service sector will be continuously arranged within the central public finance, and the central budget will be gradually increased in light of the financial situation and needs for development of the service sector." It was also required that local governments arrange special funds and guidance funds for the development of the service sector. The qualified regions would enlarge the scale of funds to support the development of the service sector.

Second, financial support of the development of the service sector should also increase. The document stated, "The People's Bank of China and other financial regulatory organs shall guide and encourage various types of financial institutions to develop financial products suitable for service enterprise, actively support qualified service enterprises to raise capital through bank loans, issuance of stocks and bonds and other channels." It also required relevant administrative departments to promote the construction of a credit security system for small and medium-size enterprises. The local funders of the development of such enterprises were required to prioritize the arrangement of subsidies or loan discounts for the development of the service sector with priority (General Office of the State Council, 2008). These financial arrangements facilitated mainly start-ups and the growth of small and medium-size game companies.

In addition to documents released by the State Council, central and local governments and various entities gave direct support to the development of online games with specific themes that, predictably, were ideology oriented rather than market oriented. For example, the Chinese Communist Youth League Shanghai Committee supported Shanda Games' development of *Xue Lei Feng* (學雷鋒) based on political role model Lei Feng (Sina Corporation, 2004a). Anticorruption is another theme of online games supported by the Chinese government. The evidence shows that in 2007, the Commission for Discipline Inspection of Haishu District, Ningbo, invested RMB¥100 thousand in developing *Qing Lian Zhan Shi* (清廉戰士). In this game, the major character must kill corrupt officials to create a world without corruption. However, this game was quickly removed from circulation because of criticism (Xinhua News Agency, 2007).

Among all themes, the war-of-resistance theme echoes the diplomatic policy of the PRC and the "major rhythm" of the propaganda line. This theme particularly relates to anti-Japanese games and their development (Interview with Yu Miao (于淼), June 13, 2010). ZQ Game, a game company in Shenzhen, developed a series of games reflecting this theme (see figures 4.2–3). The games included *War of Resistance* (大抗戰), *Kang Zhan* (抗

戰), *Kang Zhan2* (抗戰2), *Liang Jian* (亮劍), and *Liang Jian2* (亮劍2). Some of the games borrowed roles and narratives from anti-Japanese, war-theme TV drama and echoed Chinese patriotism. However, the developer made it clear that these games were aimed mainly at satisfying the authorities rather than making a profit or entering the overseas market (Interview with Huang Wanfei (黃婉斐), July 30, 2010, in Beijing).

In order to enhance China's overseas soft power by exporting games, the PRC has opened preferential tax policies to information services and other modern service industries. This move promoted the development of the information service industries. At the same time, enterprises in the creative industries were pushed to participate in international business and open international markets. These tax policies are preferential to high-tech industries and companies such as the game industry. *Opinions of the General Office of the State Council on Implementing Some Policies and Measures for Accelerating the Development of the Service Sector* stated, "The tax authority shall accelerate the pilot policy of income tax and business tax on encouraging the development of advanced technology service enterprises in Suzhou Industrial Park, [and] actively enlarge the pilot scope of preferential taxation policies for encouraging the development of productive service industries including software development, information technology, intellectual property services, engineering consulting, technology promotion, [and] outsourcing of services and modern logistics." Moreover, "the taxation authority will support service enterprises to research and develop products, [and it] can grant preferential deduction of income tax on the expenses for research and development as actually spent by enterprises according to relevant policies." The tax policies also encouraged enterprises in the information service industry to create more job opportunities and consume fewer resources: "For the service enterprises that hire a lot of workers but consume fewer resources and emit fewer pollutants, subsidies and preferential income tax rates will be granted to them based on the number of workers they have hired" (General Office of the State Council, 2008).

In contrast, an export tax rebate policy has encouraged the export of cultural products, including game products, in order to compete in the global market. The General Office of the State Council has announced that central and local governments would provide discount loans, subsidies, and incentives to support the development of cultural enterprises. The export tax rebate policy is applicable to books, newspapers, periodicals, audiovisual products, electronic publications, films, and TV dramas. Game products, which are audiovisual products, are also covered by the export tax rebate policy. For high-tech cultural enterprises that are strongly supported by the government, the taxation authorities provide a 15 percent discount on the income tax rate. The tax policies support expansion into foreign markets, technological innovation, and custom clearance for the export of cultural products and services, including games. The tax policies for the game industry are preferential to major cultural export enterprises and online game products and services with national characteristics. The policies are also in line with *Plan on Reinvigoration of the Cultural Industry*, and they help expand foreign cultural trade.

Specific to cultural and creative industries, the Chinese government has announced policies for non-public capital and encouraged the entry of non-public capital into cultural industries, including the game industry. In 2005, the State Council released *Several Opinions of the State Council on Encouraging, Supporting and Guiding the Development of Individual and Private Economy and Other Non-public Sectors of the Economy*. The main statement in the document supports the entry of non-public capital into economic development. The main points of this directive include liberalizing market access for the non-public sector, giving more tax and financial support to the non-public sector, improving social services for the non-public economy, and protecting the lawful rights and interests of enterprises in the non-public sector of the economy (Chinalawinfo, 2017c). In line with this document, the State Council released *Some Decisions of the State Council on the Entry of Non-public-owned Capital into the Cultural Industry* two months later. With a clear focus on the cultural industry, this policy stated that non–publicly owned capital would be encouraged and supported in several fields, including business sites of Internet access services, animation, and online games. This means liberalization of market access, tax and financial support, social services support, and government supervision of non-public economy are also applicable to online games and the business sites of online gaming (Chinalawinfo, 2017d).

Similar to other Asian countries, as the creative industries develop, regulations are updated to meet changes. *Regulations on the Administration of Audio and Video Products*, which was released in 2001 by the State Council of the PRC, was formally amended in 2011. These regulations apply to activities such as the publication, manufacturing, reproduction, import, sale, and leasing of audio and video products such as audio tapes, video tapes, records, compact discs, and laser disks. In the game context, the regulations apply to compact discs of console games and online games. These regulations are implemented by the government at different levels. Article 4 of this document states, "The competent publication department of the State Council shall be responsible for the supervision and administration of the publication, production, reproduction, import, wholesale, retail sale and lease of audio and video products across the country." Local governments at or above the county level are responsible for the supervision and administration of the activities listed above within their administrative regions. The above activities must be approved by the government; otherwise, they are prohibited. Article 5 of this document states, "The State shall apply a license system. No entity or individual shall, without permission, be engaged in the publication, manufacture, reproduction, import, wholesale, or retail, etc. of audio and video product."

The specific regulation about joint production affects the Hong Kong game industry. Any cooperation between Hong Kong, Macau, Taiwan, or foreign publishing entities with mainland Chinese companies is also under the supervision of a competent publication department of the State Council. On the one hand, mainland publishing entities are allowed to cooperate with organizations or individuals in Hong Kong, Macau, Taiwan, and foreign countries to manufacture audio and video products. On the other hand, such cooperation is highly controlled by the Chinese government. Without the permission of the central or regional government, entities or individuals are not allowed to cooperate with Hong Kong, Macau, Taiwan, or foreign publishing entities to manufacture or reproduce audio and video products, including video games (Chinalawinfo, 2017b).

As a rising creative cultural industry, the game industry is supported and regulated by policies at both national and regional levels. The major legislative and administrative bodies that enact game policies at the national level include the State Council, the Ministry of Culture, and the General Administration of Press and Publication. The Chinese government holds the power to approve game licenses and examine game content. In order to promote the development of the game industry, it also provides financial support and tax incentives, and it allows non-public capital to be invested. The classification of games has been discussed and studied for many years. However, the administrative authorities have not reached a consensus on a classification scheme.

REGIONAL GAME POLICIES IN CHINA

This section describes various policies in relation to the game industry implemented by administrative bodies at central, provincial, and municipal levels. Although it is impossible to compile a comprehensive list of all the policies, I have chosen classic cases to demonstrate the flexibility of their implementation in different areas of China. Some policies could be good references for the Hong Kong government in studying its own market and in competing with other Asian countries. The provincial and municipal policies for the game industry focus on financial support, tax incentives, talent training and introduction, and the establishment of public service platforms. In general, the game industry gives us the impression that there are a few strategic areas: North China, East China, South China, and Central and West China. For reasons of space and relevance, only cases in North, East, and South China are analyzed.

Beijing, the capital of China, has experienced the speediest growth in China's creative industries. Revenues from all creative industries jumped from RMB¥169.7 billion in 2010 to RMB¥317.9 billion in 2015 with an annual increase of 13 percent. It was said that amount is 13.8 percent of Beijing's entire industrial base, although we have to read such official figures with caution. In 2016, there were sixty-one publically listed companies in the creative industries with a work force of 667,000 in the sector where technology and culture are combined (Beijing Cultural Institute, 2016).

In Beijing, game policy focuses on providing financial support to the online game industry. The Beijing Municipal Bureau of Culture announced *Measures of Beijing for Supporting the Development of the Online Game Industry* in May 2010. The document stated that a special fund for Beijing cultural creative industries would be provided to support the development of the online game industry. All development, publication, and operation enterprises that were registered in Beijing and were in accordance with the direction of cultural and creative industries designed by the Beijing government were covered by the preferential policy. The privileges listed in the document extended to the products, services, and products derived from online games.

First, the Beijing Municipal Bureau of Culture would provide financial support at the stage of game development. The document indicated that the Beijing government would provide RMB¥1–2 million for the best online game products that were designed and developed by game companies in Beijing. The criteria included the following: (1) the game issue highlights Chinese characteristics and Chinese elements; (2) the game content is healthy and promotes the idea of a harmonious society; (3) the game company owns the independent intellectual property rights of the game-developing engine; (4) the game company and game products help improve the competiveness and creative capacity of the game industry; and (5) the game company has good potential for social benefits and economic benefits. These criteria are aimed at balancing internal national stability and national competitiveness overseas.

Second, the Beijing Municipal Bureau of Culture encouraged game companies to develop products with independent intellectual property rights. The Beijing government would provide RMB¥2 million to the company that developed game engines independently and produced five or more massive online games using the developed game engines. It would also provide RMB¥2 million to companies that owned independent intellectual property rights and made game products and services. The criteria included the following: (1) the annual revenue of every single online game reaches RMB¥0.1 billion or above for the game company, and the game company provides more than 100 jobs; (2) the annual revenue of the game company is RMB¥0.5 billion or above, and the game company provides more than 300 jobs; and (3) the annual revenue is RMB¥50 million or above for a mobile phone game company, and the company creates more than 100 jobs. Game companies that met any of the above criteria could be supported.

Third, company investment in infrastructure was supported by the Beijing government. RMB¥1 million would be provided to game companies that purchased and leased RMB¥40 million in servers and bandwidths. Mobile phone game companies that purchased RMB¥20 million worth of servers would receive RMB¥0.5 million. The Beijing government would also subsidize game companies that purchased or constructed 2,000 square meters or more of office space in Beijing's National Online Game Industrial Base.

Fourth, which is relevant to the thesis of this book, the export to overseas markets was also encouraged by the game policies established in Beijing. A bonus of RMB¥2 million would be provided to a game company whose export volume was US$8 million or more. An additional criterion was that the game company should own the independent intellectual property rights (Beijing Municipal Bureau of Culture, 2010).

In addition to financial support, the Beijing government included talent in the evaluation of professional titles. In 2012, the Beijing Municipal Bureau of Human Resources and Social Security announced that a new evaluation system would be established for game talent. The officials argued that the majority of game talent was young, and they entered the game industry very early. Thus the evaluation system would emphasize practice and performance rather than educational background or degree of education. The proposed evaluation system comprised three levels. Individuals could achieve professional titles through examinations or assessments. The system would help promote training in the game industry. The evaluation system would lead to fewer workers and fewer material costs to enterprises in evaluating game talent. It would also promote the mobility of individuals with qualified and certified game talent.

In addition to financial support and talent training, the Beijing government implemented *Measures for Administration of Guarantee Fund of Beijing Cultural and Creative Industries* and *Measures for Supporting the National Online Game and Animation Industry (Beijing) Development Base*. These measures included strategies to promote the development of the game industry in Beijing and create a cluster effect in the core online game industrial base.

East China is the most developed region in the country. A great number of enterprises and workers in the cultural and creative industries are located in this region. The major cities in East China—namely, Shanghai, Suzhou, and Hangzhou—provide preferential policies for the game industry.

Statistics show that Shanghai's GDP ranks first among Chinese cities, reaching RMB¥2,010.13 billion (Elivecity.cn, 2013). Because Shanghai is one of the most important and fastest developing centers of the game industry, its government established the China National Center for Developing the

Animation, Cartoon and Game Industry. In 2004, the market size of the online game industry in Shanghai was RMB¥1.6 billion. Five years later, the market size was RMB¥10.03 billion. According to the *2009 White Paper of China Online Game Market*, the online game industry in Shanghai took about 40 percent of the market share of the entire nation (Xinhua News Agency, 2009b). At the end of 2009, there were 96 qualified and licensed online game companies, which accounted for 20 percent of the 499 game companies in China. The total amount of registered capital of the 96 game companies in Shanghai was RMB¥1.6 billion. Among the 96 game companies in Shanghai, 58 were operating online games, while others were in the preliminary stages of research and development.

In Shanghai, game companies operated more than 180 online games (excluding online Flash games), in which domestic games accounted for 78 percent (140 games). The revenue from domestic games was 60 percent of total revenue, which was in line with the proportion of domestic and imported online games in the national market. In 2009, the export volume of online games produced in Shanghai reached US$27 million, which was 25 percent of the total export volume. The major overseas markets for Shanghai online games were Hong Kong, Taiwan, Korea, Japan, Thailand, Singapore, Vietnam, the Philippines, and Russia.

According to an interview with Ren Huajian (任花建), director of the Cultural Industry Research Center of the Shanghai Academy of Social Science, effective incentive policies and a platform of industrial public service contributed to the rapid development of the game industry in Shanghai. Regarding the incentive policies, Shanghai launched *Supportive and Incentive Measures of Shanghai Animation and Game Industries* in 2010. The principles of the policy include guiding the animation and game industry, fostering outstanding companies and original products, complementing industrial chains, and promoting the development of the animation and game industry. In this document, "online game enterprises" are defined as enterprises that are registered in Shanghai, develop online games, and provide operation services.

The first main point of the document is that it encourages green online games and games with themes that promote traditional Chinese culture. The Shanghai government will provide up to RMB¥0.2 million to each outstanding company with RMB¥10 million or above in annual revenue. It will award up to RMB¥0.1 million to each outstanding company that develops serious online games with RMB¥0.2 million or more in annual revenue. The amount of RMB¥0.1 million will be provided to each outstanding mobile phone game company with RMB¥0.5 million or more in annual revenue. The second point is that the document encourages game companies to develop derived products along a game value chain, such as films, videos, and toys. The Shanghai government will provide up to RMB¥0.3 million to each outstanding company that creates RMB¥5 million or above in annual revenue from derived products (Shanghai Municipal Administration of Culture, Radio, Film, and TV, 2012a).

The export of original online games and derived products is also highly supported by the Shanghai government. It provides up to RMB¥0.2 million to outstanding exported derived game products with RMB¥2 million or more in revenue. It also encourages Shanghai game companies to participate in overseas game exhibitions. The registration fee and exhibition fee are partially sponsored by the government (Shanghai Municipal Administration of Culture, Radio, Film, & TV, 2012b). Regarding the platform of industrial public service, Ren described three major types of platforms in Shanghai, including animation and online game platforms, copyright transaction platforms, and cultural service and trade platforms. Supporting services, such as bonding companies, microcredit companies, and certification and inspection companies, would be optimized if all these platforms were connected. The investment environment would be better if all these supporting service companies were connected. The government is confident that investors will come to Shanghai if the investment environment is attractive and promising enough.

An interview with an official of the Shanghai Municipal Administration of Culture, Radio, Film, and TV yielded information about policies governing the investment of joint capital from mainland China and Hong Kong. As opposed to foreign capital, the central government and the Shanghai government have a more welcoming attitude toward Hong Kong capital. If mainland enterprises control greater than 51 percent of the venture, Hong Kong capital is able to participate directly. Although games produced by joint ventures of Hong Kong and mainland companies have recently been regarded as game products produced outside China, the situation has adjusted as policies have changed. As in other industries, China's game industry is gradually allowing the investment of Hong Kong capital.

The game policies of South China should be given particular attention here not only because the Pearl River Delta area is one of the densest and fastest-growing economic regions of China but also because its proximity to Hong Kong engenders the latter's hope to develop its game industry. South China is the center of China's online game industry. The best-known online game enterprises are located in this area, including NetEase Games, Kingsoft Games, and Optisp. These companies initiated the development of online games and still possess strong potential (Muynck, 2012). The largest game company in China, Tencent, is headquartered in Shenzhen. In mid-2017, Tencent announced that it received an annual revenue of RMB¥49.5 billion from the mainland market, of which RMB¥22.8 billion was from online games (*Apple Daily*, 2017).

Since the introduction of China's policies of reform and opening, Shenzhen has become China's first and most successful special economic zone. In

2012, Shenzhen's GDP was RMB¥1.295 billion, which was the fourth highest in China (Elivecity.cn, 2013). The modern creative industry in Shenzhen has boomed in recent decades. According to *Opinions on Supporting the Development of Animation and Game Industries*, which was released in August 2005, Shenzhen's municipal government has prioritized the development of the animation and game industry. The concrete measures included building creative clusters, providing financial subsidies and tax incentives, and establishing training organizations.

First, the local government built creative parks in different districts of Shenzhen, such as Tianmian Design City, OCT Loft, Luohu Creative Plaza, Nanshan Park, Shenzhen Animation Town, Shenzhen-Hong Kong Animation & Game Fostering Base, Shenzhen Animation Street, Yijing Animation Park, Bao'an Arts Zone 22, and No. 8 Zhongkang Road. These parks are creative clusters that attract creative talent, especially young designers and developers. These clusters also serve as platforms for information, exhibition, and communication, and they provide value-added services such as copyright transactions and investment consulting services to designers and enterprises in the parks (Muynck, 2012). Different sectors of the Shenzhen government, the municipal government, and district governments collaborate to support public platforms for technology services in industrial bases. The projects in industrial bases are subsidized by a special fund. The maximal subsidy for each project is RMB¥3 million (or 10 percent of the actual investment). The Shenzhen government will also provide three-year subsidies for new enterprises in municipal, provincial, or national cultural industrial bases.

Second, the Shenzhen government provides subsidies to qualified game companies and relevant enterprises. Animation and game enterprises recommended by the Shenzhen Municipal Office of Cultural Industries and recognized by national and provincial special funds for cultural industries can apply for a one-to-one matching grant. Organizations that host national or international exhibitions of the animation and game industry are subsidized according to the cultural area. Local animation and game companies that attend national and international exhibitions in China are also subsidized. Original animation and games produced in Shenzhen that receive important international, national, and provincial prizes are also awarded. Publishers of original animation and games are awarded up to RMB¥1 million according to sales revenue from these products.

Third, tax incentives are provided to qualified animation and game companies in Shenzhen. Game companies that are officially certified or rated as high-tech or software companies enjoy preferential tax policies. The importers of advanced technology and facilities are also favored by the above policies.

Fourth, compared with the governments of other cities, the Shenzhen government puts more emphasis on talent training. Shenzhen policies encourage companies to establish training organizations to foster game talent. For example, Shenzhen Perfect Space Education is a training institution that provides courses in game design and game development. To take advantage of advanced technology in the game industries of other countries, the best animation and game talent in Shenzhen is selected for training abroad, which is fully supported by public funds. Shenzhen *hukou* (permanent residence) is given to individuals with game talent, especially those in creative, market development, and executive positions. The quotas of Shenzhen *hukou* are given to professionals who hold bachelor's degrees or higher and are employed by animation and game companies. Preferential medical insurance, education, and low-rent housing are offered to individuals who hold master's degrees or higher and those who achieve senior professional positions. The Shenzhen government also encourages communication and collaboration between Shenzhen and Hong Kong. Concrete measures include (1) encouraging Hong Kong game companies to establish branches in Shenzhen and (2) encouraging Hong Kong animation and game enterprises to move their developing, training, and marketing departments to Shenzhen. The Shenzhen government also attempts to guarantee Hong Kong game companies in Shenzhen the same status as mainland companies.

Although Shenzhen is the closest geographically to Hong Kong of any Chinese city, Guangzhou, the capital of the southern Guangzhou Province, is the closest linguistically to Hong Kong: both share the same Cantonese language. In 2012, Guangzhou had the third-highest GDP in China (RMB¥1,355.12 billion, an increase of 10.5 percent; Elivecity.cn, 2013). The growing online game and animation industries contribute to Guangzhou's GDP. Guangzhou is one of the first-tier national online game and animation industrial bases. In addition to being a national industrial base, Guangzhou has established several online game and animation industrial areas in the Tianhe and Huangpu districts (Li, Zhao, & Tian, 2008). The local government therefore provides its full support in making Guangzhou the hub of the game industry in China.

According to *Regulations of Guangzhou on Further Supporting the Development of Software and Animation Industries*, which was released in 2005, the online game industry includes the software industry. The regulations contain twenty-nine articles that cover major points such as a special fund, professional certification, original game incentives, worker training, intellectual property rights, market regulations, international collaboration, and competition.

In 2007, the Guangzhou government established a special fund to support the development of software and animation companies with approximately RMB¥0.15 billion in annual financial support. The municipal bureau of technology, the municipal development and reform commission, and the municipal bureau of finance contribute to the fund. This special fund was established to encourage investment in software and animation industries, award senior technicians and executive talent, and support the construction of software and animation industrial bases.

Second, the Guangzhou government rewards companies that invest in software and animation industries. For each software or animation enterprise or research institution with more than RMB¥10 million in investments, 5 percent of the total investment (up to RMB¥3 million) is awarded. For each software or animation enterprise or research institution with more than RMB¥30 million of investments, 6 percent of the total investment (up to RMB¥5 million) is awarded.

Third, the Guangzhou government encourages loan companies to provide loan guarantees to software and animation enterprises. Up to RMB¥0.5 million is awarded to each loan guarantee company that provides guarantees over one year.

Fourth, the local government emphasizes the professional certification of enterprises. Software companies that receive ISO 9001 certification are awarded up to RMB¥50 thousand. Software companies that pass capacity maturity model/capacity maturity model integration (CMM/CMMI2), CMM/CMMI3, CMM/CMMI4, or CMM/CMMI5 are awarded RMB¥0.2 million, RMB¥0.3 million, RMB¥0.4 million, or RMB¥0.5 million, respectively.

Fifth, the production of original games and animation is encouraged. Each original game licensed by national administrative bodies is awarded RMB¥50,000–200,000 according to the quality and the influence of the game.

Sixth, technological innovation is highly emphasized by the Guangzhou government. The government helps improve public platforms of research and development and promotes enterprises' capability in technological innovation. The municipal bureau of technology provides financial subsidies for important software and animation development projects and the joint projects of enterprises, universities, and research institutions.

Seventh, the introduction and training of workers is included in Guangzhou's game policies. The municipal bureau of technology provides RMB¥0.2 million and RMB¥0.3 million to each software park or software enterprise, respectively, that offers postdoctoral positions. Vocational education and professional training are emphasized. Individuals who are trained in certified software and animation training centers, subsequently receive senior certificates and work in the software and animation profession in Guangzhou are subsidized by 30 percent of the training fee (up to RMB¥10 thousand) by the industrial development fund. The fund also provides housing subsidies (up to RMB¥50 thousand) and Guangzhou *hukou* to attract domestic and foreign professionals to work in the software and animation industries in that city. In addition, a preferential individual income tax rate is provided to attract game talent.

Eighth, the Guangzhou government promotes international collaboration and competition. The industrial development fund subsidizes enterprises that participate in international exhibitions and project negotiations abroad and are recognized by the Bureau of Foreign Trade and Economic Cooperation of Guangzhou Municipality. It also encourages enterprises to approach the international market. Companies that export original games or animations can apply for special funding from the bureau (Guangzhou Municipal Government, 2005).

CULTURAL CLUSTERS IN CHINA

In China, national and regional policies commonly include the establishment of cultural clusters, which are geographic concentrations of companies and institutions in connection to creative or cultural industries (Fung & Erni, 2013). The concept was introduced by Michael Porter (1998), who was one of the first scholars to suggest that the clustering of interlinked industries is important for competition. Today, the concept of clusters has a much wider meaning. Table 4.1 summarizes some important definitions of the concept.

Today, the theoretical concept of clustering is strategically applied by governments to promote their creative industries. China has widely applied the concept of cultural clusters to its development of cultural policies. Dating to the formation of the PRC in the early 1950s, the concept of industry clusters has a long history in China (China Briefing, 2012), and the legacy of industry clusters have now been extended to creative or cultural clusters on different levels. Although the number of cultural clusters on the national, provincial, and municipal level is huge, no updated statistics are available. However, several business incubators—mainly high-tech and digital—have been founded in China, many of which are located in these clusters. In 2015, there were 2,530 incubators related to technology, and they represented a creative space for 4,875 various cultural industries, which was the largest establishment of this kind in the world (KKnews, 2016). Today, on the national level, under the MOC, these cultural clusters are often called "Technological Parks," "Science Parks," or "Cultural Industrial Parks." This is where related creative industries such as film, animation and online games are housed with their software and information technology industry counterparts.

Cultural clusters are based on various models. Some cultural clusters specialize in a particular cultural industry, but this is rarely the case in China. The most common type of cultural cluster in China involves companies along the same value chain that produce, sell, or distribute similar cultural

Table 4.1.   Defining "Cluster"

Study	Definition
Morfessis (1994)	A high concentration of companies in a specific region.
OCED Focus Group (1996)	Reduced-scale national innovation systems. It is a network of industries maintaining knowledge linkages and interdependencies between actors in networks of production and consumption.
Roelandt and Hertog (1999)	A network of production of strongly interdependent firms correlated to other value-adding institutions such as research institutes, knowledge intensive business services, and agencies in production chains for maximizing economic benefit and reducing investment risk.
Simmie and Sennett (1999)	Driven by the market demand, clusters operate in economic-based and manufacturing companies that cooperate with other related industries such as logistics and sales.
Porter (2000)	Geographical concentrations of interconnected companies, specialized suppliers, service providers, firms in related industries, and associated institutions (e.g., universities, standards, agencies, and trade associations) in a particular field that both compete and cooperate.
UNIDO (2001)	A geographical agglomeration of production companies in a specific or relative business encountering risk and opportunity at the same stage.
Cooke and Huggins (2002)	Enterprises with standardized or vertical correlation-based business from both upstream and downstream in a production chain, including infrastructure for supporting business development.
Zacarelli (2004) (cited in de Cunha and de Cunha [2005])	Inclusion of characteristics related to technology, competitiveness, environmental and cultural sustainability and quality of life, and synergies in systematic relations.
Cooke and Lazzeretti (2007)	A system of relations set in a territorially bounded area, which integrates the process of valorization of material and immaterial cultural resources with infrastructures and different productive sectors associated with the process itself.

Source: Table modified from Fung & Erni, 2013.

products such as software, digital products, and digital games. In theory, the companies in the cluster function as units in the production chain. By working together, they maximize the competitive advantages of the industry involved. However, in China, most of these clusters are directly or indirectly financed by the state, and this differs from models in Europe and America in which cultural clusters are financed by multiple sources and customer preferences are prioritized (Brooks & Kushner, 2001). In this study, I made multiple observations in these creative hubs. On one site visit, I talked to the management company Dotman Digital Entertainment, which has a central office in a creative hub. In most of the clusters that I visited, after the formation of the hub and the settlement of the cultural industries in it, the management companies became invisible and could not be traced easily.

Dotman Digital Entertainment manages Shijingshan's Beijing Cyber Recreation District (CRD), a creative hub on the west side of Beijing. It comprises eight centers, including the Online Game Incubation Center; R&D Center of Games for Mobile Phones; Digital Industry Information Center; Experience Show and Athletic Center; Training Center; Animation Center; Digital Trading Center; and Game Testing and Promotion Center (Fung & Erni, 2013). In the hub are well-compartmentalized, functional districts: an entertainment district, a recreation district, and a district of high-tech innovation, which is a training site. In practice, in the CRD, different units rarely interact. I observed interactions between animation companies and a game company, but not within the industrial chain. In an interview, the deputy manager of Dotman, Hao Yong (郝勇), revealed some interesting facts about how the cluster operated. According to Hao, Shijingshan is a "logical concept" comprising an area of 1.33 square miles that was especially created for cultural creativity and digital entertainment. Dotman used to attract creative industries to rent space in the cluster, but rentals were now handled by the government, and Dotman's new mission was to create and manage a virtual economic zone to serve the industries in the CRD, a responsibility that ranged from facilitating talent exchanges between universities and the industries in the hub to setting up research space in a reserved area in the CRD (Interview July 19, 2010, in Beijing). Among all the advantages of the CRD that Hao discussed, the greatest attraction for companies was *hukou*, or the granting of permanent residence to professionals in the companies that settled in the hub. In view of the unpredictable conditions of labor in the game industry, *hukou* provides the professional with a lifelong sanctuary.

I also visited a hub in the Shangdi area where the Shangdi Information Creative Base was established in 1991. The authorities attempted to transform this area into a "Dreamworld" of China where there would be clusters of creative industries and IT industries, including Lenovo, International Business Machines (IBM), Huawei, General Motors, and China's largest search engine, Baidu. Game companies such as Perfect World and Guangyu Games also located their headquarters in this hub. Interestingly, my interviews with the staff of Perfect World were conducted in a canteen on the first floor of the office. Although the interviews did not yield much data about this cluster, the setting of the canteen led to insights. With the exception of the canteen, no restaurant existed in the hub of high-tech office buildings. The canteen seemed to serve decent Chinese meals at prices comparable to those in town, and the staff, which included programmers in jeans and senior management in suits, were all in the canteen, where the tables were less than three feet apart. In short, the entire workforce of the hub was crowded into this small space, which was surrounded by four gray, largely undecorated walls. Based on this, I would say that a cultural cluster is no more than an "upgraded" high-tech workplace that differs little from industrial factories. In fact, the purpose is similar: maximize the efficiency of digital production and not the quality of life of creative workers.

Companies that locate in a cluster do so for pragmatic reasons, and they neither interact with nor participate in a value chain, which is counter to the concept. They value the subsidies of state and the tax reductions given by the district government or the cluster. Hence their motives raise the question of why the industries in these cultural clusters should be privileged. Indeed, based on the findings of my study, it is doubtful whether cultural development is indeed speeded up by the establishment of cultural clusters. However, from the authorities' point of view, these clusters serve to boost the economy and the investment of capital in a district. Thus there is a symbiotic economic relationship among the state, the municipality, and private capital. In the course of collaboration, cultural clusters become platforms that legalize the state's intervention in the economy and a legitimized means of maximizing the state's interests.

Furthermore, in relation to the thesis of East Asian rivalry, cultural clusters as well as other financial supports serve the state's political agenda to compete with other countries in a contemporary, geopolitical arena. Joseph Nye (2004) called "soft power" the power of a nation to demonstrate its economic power and to ally with global capital to expand its influence. In the context of the competitive geopolitics of East Asia, culture, as a main currency of soft power, is an alternative—although possibly inferior—way to demonstrate China's strong status, in addition to military action and diplomacy. In this sense, cultural clusters can be regarded as an easy and proven way of increasing GDP in terms of the growth of creative industries and of manufacturing cultural exports to enhance the soft power of the state.

However, China is not alone in establishing cultural clusters. Other countries and regions, such as Hong Kong, Taiwan and Singapore, have long-established technological parks. As we'll see in the next chapter, countries such as South Korea have been active in establishing cultural clusters for the sake of promoting national soft power. In other words, echoing the old Chinese saying about the planned economy, despite the game industry and technological advancement, a state-planned action to establish industrial complexes or cultural clusters is the most direct means of achieving the targeted goals of a nation. Instead of traditional, heavily polluting industrial goods, the planned economy fosters the production of intangible digital cultural goods such as online games in order to compete globally.

CHINA'S CULTURAL POLICIES AS A REFERENCE

This chapter has presented a state-driven model of the creative industries, particularly the game industry. However, the operation of the game industry does not follow the logic of supply and demand. It seems that much of state cultural policy is a catalyst for new development or an accelerator of economic growth through either financial subsidies or the formation of cultural clusters. The policies of the central government are designed to work in tandem with regional authoritative entities that provide preferential policies to support the development of the game industry in their regions. These policies vary little. Financially, they provide special funding and tax incentives for game development. Game products that have independent intellectual property rights, that represent a sound investment in infrastructure, and that can be successfully exported to overseas markets are the criteria for support. The censorship of games is not uncommon because the development of such creative industries—or the expansion of GDP—must not upset the state's interest. When the national interest is guaranteed, the state uses public funds to support the game industry. Principles of fairness, equity, and a socialist economy are mentioned after each policy, whether national or regional, is implemented.

Nevertheless, although the HKSAR is a part of China, favorable national cultural policies do not apply to the HKSAR although the Shenzhen municipal government is inclined to cooperate with Hong Kong. This lack of inclusion further confirms arguments I made earlier: China as a cultural market for Hong Kong is only a discourse of the HKSAR government and a hegemonic fantasy of the Hong Kong public. It seems that the stronger China's cultural policy—which serves to expand its game industry—the bigger the threat to Hong Kong. In short, China's future cultural policies might constitute a strong force for conquering markets in East Asia, including those of Hong Kong. Such policies would further marginalize Hong Kong's game industry and its ability to import products to China. First, the expectation that China's cultural policy might bolster Hong Kong's game and creative industries is naive and unrealistic. Second, from Hong Kong's point of view, East Asian rivalry, which is mainly conceived as Hong Kong's competition with Korea, should be restructured to include China. Third, as I emphasize repeatedly, the argument that China's cultural economy can benefit Hong Kong is utterly unsubstantiated and is upheld by the HKSAR to highlight the political significance of China for Hong Kong, to frame it as a viable social policy, and to create the false hope that Hong Kong will share in China's rising economy.

REFERENCES

17173.com. (2010). Ministry of Culture: Rating system of online games is not included in plans of administration [文化部：網游分級並未列入管理工作計劃]. Retrieved from http://news.17173.com/content/2010-01-27/20100127121025184.shtml.

Ahearne, J., & Bennett, O. (2013). *Intellectuals and cultural policy*. London: Routledge.

Apple Daily. (2017). Tencent annual report: King of stock profit reached 60 percent in the first season, stock price reaches HK$263 in European trading period [蘋果日報 (2017) 騰訊業績 股王首季多賺近六成 歐洲時段股價升見263元]. Retrieved from http://hk.apple.nextmedia.com/realtime/finance/20170517/56705683.

Bashford, C., & Langley, L. (Eds.). (2000). *Music and British culture, 1785–1914: Essays in honour of Cyril Ehrlich*. Oxford: Oxford University Press.

Beijing Municipal Bureau of Culture [北京市文化局]. (2010). Measures of Beijing for supporting the development of the online game industry [北京市關於支持網絡遊戲產業發展的實施辦法.]. Retrieved from http://games.ifeng.com/netgame/yejiexiaoxi/detail_2010_05/20/1535627_1.shtml.

Beijing Cultural Institute [北京市文化創意产促進中心北京文化創意产业发展白皮书]. (2016). Beijing cultural and creative industries development white paper (2016): Manuscript 1. Retrieved from http://www.sohu.com/a/120026319_473338.

Bennett, O. (1996). *Cultural policy and the crisis of legitimacy: Entrepreneurial answers in the United Kingdom*. Warwick, UK: University of Warwick Centre for the Study of Cultural Policy.

Brooks, A., & Kushner, R. (2001). Cultural districts and urban development. *International Journal of Arts Management, 3*(2), 4–15.

Central Committee of the Communist Party of China [中共中央]. (1995). The central committee of the Communist party of China's recommendation of the ninth five-year plan for national economic and social development [中共中央關於制定國民經濟和社會發展第九個五年計劃的建議]. Retrieved from http://cpc.people.com.cn/GB/64184/64186/66686/4494285.html.

China Briefing. (2012). China's industrial clusters. Retrieved from http://www.china-briefing.com/news/2012/02/23/chinas-industry-clusters.html.

China Copyright Office & General Administration of Press and Publication [CCO & GAPP] [國家版權局、新聞出版總署]. (2009). Notice of the general administration of press and publication, the national copyright administration and the office of the national work group for "combating pornography and illegal publications" on implementing the provisions of the state council on "three determinations" and the relevant explanations of the state commission office for public sector reform and further strengthening the administration of the pre-approval of online games and examination and approval of imported online games [新闻出版总署、国家版权局、全国"扫黄打非"工作小组办公室关于贯彻落实国务院《"三定"规定》和中央编办有关解释，进一步加强网络游戏前置审批和进口网络游戏审批管理的通知]. Retrieved from http://en.pkulaw.cn/display.aspx?id=8055&lib=law&SearchKeyword=&SearchCKeyword=oX1ktBw6BrApercent3d.

Chinalawinfo. (2017a). Provision of the state council for further making perfect economic policy on culture [國務院關於進一步完善文化經濟政策的若干規定]. Retrieved from http://www.lawinfochina.com/display.aspx?lib=law&id=6293&CGid=.

Chinalawinfo. (2017b). Regulations on the administration of audio and video products [音像製品管理條例]. Retrieved from http://en.pkulaw.cn/display.aspx?id=2242&lib=law&SearchKeyword=Regulations on the Administration of Audio and Video Products&SearchCKeyword=mc percent2frPBmvuUE percent3d.

Chinalawinfo. (2017c). Several opinions of the State Council on encouraging, supporting and guiding the development of individual and private economy and other non-public sectors of the economy [國務院關於鼓勵支持和引導個體私營等非公有制經濟發展的若干意見]. Retrieved from http://en.pkulaw.cn/display.aspx?id=3977&lib=law&SearchKeyword=&SearchCKeyword=nRl percent2fZd8ZjOly0bLFGe1XYpr5 percent2bJpj83Oa.

Chinalawinfo. (2017d). Some decisions of the State Council on the entry of non-public-owned capital into the cultural industry [國務院關於非公有制資本進入文化產業的若干決定].

Retrieved from http://en.pkulaw.cn/display.aspx?id=4202&lib=law&SearchKeyword=&SearchCKeyword=2Opercent2fEyn7YrXpercent2bVlWi1jNN7YApercent3dpercent3d.

Cooke, P., & Huggins, R. (2002). High technology clustering in Cambridge. In Amin, S. Goglio, & F. Sforzi (Eds.), *The institutions of local development* (pp. 34–46). London: IGU.

Cooke, P., & Lazzeretti, L. (Eds.). (2007). *Creative cities, cultural clusters and local economic development.* Cheltenham, UK: Edward Edgar.

Craik, Jr. (2007). *Re-visioning arts and cultural policy: Current impasses and future directions.* Canberra: Australian National University Press.

Da Cunha, S. K., & da Cunha, J. C. (2005). Tourism cluster competitiveness and sustainability: Proposal for systematic model to measure the impact of tourism on local development. *Brazilian Administration Review, 2*(2), pp. 47–62.

Dogame. (2013). Game talents of Dogame participated in the fifth annual convention of online game talent in China [Dogame遊戲人才參加第五屆中國動漫遊戲人才年會]. Retrieved from http://edu.dogame.com.cn/zhinan_show.php?id=542 .

Elivecity.cn. (2013). 2012 GDP ranking of Chinese cities [2012年中國城市GDP排名]. Retrieved from http://www.elivecity.cn/html/jingjifz/731.html.

Evans, G. (2001). *Culture planning: An urban renaissance?* London: Routledge.

Fang, D. (2004). Classification scheme for online games. Retrieved from http://www.scmp.com/article/477843/classification-scheme-online-games.

Frey, B. (2013). *Arts and economics: Analysis and cultural policy* (2nd ed.). Berlin: Springer-Verlag.

Fung, A. (2016). Strategizing for creative industries in China: Contradictions and tension in nation branding. *International Journal of Communication, 10*, 3004–3021.

Fung, A., & Erni, J. (2013). Cultural clusters and cultural industries in China. *Inter-Asia Cultural Studies, 14*(4), 644–656.

Fung, A., & Liao, S. (2015). China. In M. Wolf (Ed.), *Video games around the world* (pp. 119–135). Boston, MA: MIT Press.

Games.china.com.cn. (2012). The introduction of online game industry in SISPARK [蘇州工業園區遊戲產業概況]. Retrieved from http://www.china.com.cn/games/2012-04/11/content_25112318.htm.

General Administration of Press and Publication [新聞出版總署]. (2009). Notice of the general administration of press and publication on strengthening the administration of examination and approval of imported online games [新聞出版總署關於加強對進口網絡遊戲審批管理的通知]. Retrieved from http://en.pkulaw.cn/display.aspx?id=8095&lib=law&SearchKeyword=&SearchCKeyword=oX1ktBw6BrA percent3d.

General Office of the Hubei Provincial Government [湖北省政府辦公廳]. (2010). Interim measures of administration for a special fund for supporting animation industries in Hubei [湖北省扶持動漫產業發展專項資金管理辦法（試行）]. Retrieved from http://wenku.baidu.com/link?url=gv88UjqhAs3KdHxRcKKUgG6euwlHLbHfy2wJSvZ0zMrqa6iZAcnTUUlStocanQYojx2oM4LYWz-8sxySjSXk-tuoNfEih77wNvnZE8GIwXO.

General Office of the State Council [國務院辦公廳]. (2008). Opinions of the general office of the state council on implementing some policies and measures for accelerating the development of the service sector [國務院辦公廳關於加快發展服務業若干政策措施的實施意見]. Retrieved from http://en.pkulaw.cn/display.aspx?id=6715&lib=law&SearchKeyword=&SearchCKeyword=kpercent2btMCniCzOHJEa9eNFvFNzSN9uZiRDnxfpercent2fIhZGL8IU4percent3d.

General Office of the State Council [國務院辦公廳]. (2009). Plan on reinvigoration of the cultural industry [文化產業振興規劃]. Retrieved from http://en.pkulaw.cn/display.aspx?id=8279&lib=law&SearchKeyword=&SearchCKeyword=2Opercent2fEyn7YrXpercent2bVlWi1jNN7YApercent3dpercent3d.

Gray, C. (1996). Comparing cultural policy: A reformulation. *European Journal of Cultural Policy, 2*(2), 213–222.

Gray, C. (2009) Managing cultural policy: Pitfalls and prospects. *Public Administration, 87*(3), 574–585.

Guangzhou Municipal Government [廣州市政府]. (2005). Regulations of Guangzhou on further supporting the development of the software and animation industries [廣州市進一步扶持軟件和動漫產業發展的若干規定]. Retrieved from http://baike.baidu.com/link?url=rqJKI3UUsKsufWYwdj1u07WO9zYNV9qvSmbGC_xdCrk2MzPOK0RqFEUjH8Y2FaSewivhofKFXflT7H_DvS3j0_.

Hangzhou Binjiang District Government [杭州市濱江區人民政府]. (2009). Opinions on encouraging the development of the cultural and creative industries [關於鼓勵文化創意產業發展的若干意見]. Retrieved from http://www.hhtz.gov.cn/ResourceFileData/doc/3b0d1b1d-6030-4b1e-96c6-ecf468f73bb3.doc.

Hangzhou Municipal Government [杭州市民人政府]. (2005). Opinions on encouraging and supporting the development of the animation and game industry [杭州市人民政府辦公廳關於鼓勵和扶持動漫遊戲產業發展的若干意見]. Retrieved from http://www.hangzhou.gov.cn/main/zwdt/ztzj/dsjdm/xgwj/T162467.shtml.

Hesmondhalgh, D. (2012). *The cultural industries* (3rd ed.). Thousand Oaks, CA: Sage Publications.

Hu, J. [胡錦濤]. (2007). Report at the 17th National Congress of the CPC [胡錦在在中國共產黨第十七次全國人民代表大會上的報告]. Retrieved from http://news.xinhuanet.com/english/2007-10/24/content_6938749.htm.

Hubei Provincial Party Committee & Hubei Provincial Government [中共湖北省委、湖北省人民政府]. (2009). Some opinions on promoting cultural development and prosperity [中共湖北省委湖北省人民政府關於推動文化大發展大繁榮的若干意見]. Retrieved from http://www.360doc.com/content/12/0229/23/7907551_190693495.shtml.

Keane, M. (2007). *Made in China: The great new leap forward*. New York: Routledge.

Kern, P., Smits, Y., & Wang, D. (2011). Mapping the cultural and creative sectors in the EU and China: A working paper in support of the development of an EU–China Cultural and Creative Industries (CCIs) platform. Retrieved from http://www.marcasepatentes.pt/files/collections/pt_PT/1/178/IPR2percent20-percent20Mappingpercent20thepercent20Culturalpercent20andpercent20Creativepercent20Sectorspercent20inpercent20thepercent20EUpercent20andpercent20China.pdf.

KKnews. (2016). Figures about co-working space announced, China has already become the nation with the most incubators [眾創空間50強公佈，中國已成全球孵化器數量最多的國家]. Retrieved from https://kknews.cc/zh-hk/finance/66pa2p.html.

Li, X., Zhao, C., & Tian, J. [李霞, 趙崇煦, & 田靜]. (2008). The development and strategies of online game and animation industries in Guangzhou: A comparison with Beijing, Shanghai and Chengdu [廣州網絡遊戲動漫產業的發展現狀與對策研究——兼與北京、上海與成都等城市進行比較分析]. *South China Review* [珠江經濟], *2*, 66–75.

Liu, X. (2014). The politics of Chinese digital games. *Yazhou Zhoukan, 28*(5). Retrieved from http://www.yzzk.com/cfm/content_archive.cfm?id=1390449695448&docissue=2014-05&utm_source=twitterfeed&utm_medium=twitter.

McGuigan, J. (2004). *Rethinking cultural policy*. London: Open University Press.

McGuigan, J., & Gilmore, A. (2002). The millennium dome: Sponsoring, meaning and visiting. *International Journal of Cultural Policy, 8*, 1–20.

Ministry of Culture of the People's Republic of China. (2010). Interim measures for the administration of online games [網絡遊戲管理暫行辦法]. Retrieved from http://en.pkulaw.cn/display.aspx?id=8179&lib=law&SearchKeyword=&SearchCKeyword=oX1ktBw6BrApercent3d.

Ministry of Culture & Ministry of Information Industry. (2005). Some opinions of the Ministry of Culture and the Ministry of Information Industry on the development and administration of net games [文化部、信息產業部關於網絡遊戲發展和管理的若干意見]. Retrieved from http://en.pkulaw.cn/display.aspx?id=4424&lib=law&SearchKeyword=&SearchCKeyword=oX1ktBw6BrApercent3d.

Morfessis, I. (1994). A cluster-analytic approach to identifying and developing state target industries: The case of Arizona. *Economy Development Review* (Spring), 33–57.

Muynck, B. D. (2012). Pearl River delta (PRD). Retrieved from http://www.culturalexchange-cn.nl/node/2190.

National People's Congress [第十屆全國人民代表大會]. (2001). Report on the 10th five-year plan for national economic and social development [中華人民共和國國民經濟和社會發展第十個五年規劃綱要]. Retrieved from http://www.gov.cn/english/official/2005-07/29/content_18334.htm.

National People's Congress [第十一屆全國人民代表大會]. (2006). Report on the 11th five-year plan for national economic and social development [中華人民共和國國民經濟和社會發展第十一個五年規劃綱要]. Retrieved from http://en.ndrc.gov.cn/hot/t20060529_71334.htm.

National People's Congress [第十二屆全國人民代表大會]. (2011). Report on the 12th five-year plan for national economic and social development [中華人民共和國國民經濟和社會發展第十二個五年規劃綱要]. Retrieved from http://www.moa.gov.cn/fwllm/jjps/201103/t20110317_1949003.htm.

O' Hagan, J. W. (1998). Art museums: Collections, deaccessioning and donations. *Journal of Cultural Economics, 22*(2), 197–207.

People.cn. (2010). Are online games full of violence and pornography? [網絡游戲是不是充滿暴力和色情的洪水猛獸？] *China Economic Weekly* [中国经济周刊]. Retrieved from http://npc.people.com.cn/BIG5/28320/182119/182337/11007756.html.

Pine, J., & Gilmore, J. (1999). *The experience economy*. Boston: Harvard Business School Press.

Porter, M. E. (1998). Clusters and the new economics of competition. *Harvard Business Review, 76*(6), 77–90.

Porter, M. E. (2000). Location, competition, and economic development: Local clusters in a global economy. *Economic Development Quarterly, 14*, 15–34.

Roelandt, T. J. A., & Hertog, P. D. (1999). Cluster analysis and cluster-based policy making in OECD countries: An introduction to the theme (pp. 9–23). *Boosting innovation: The cluster approach*. Paris: OECD Publishing.

Rossiter, N. (2016). *Software, infrastructure, labor: A media theory of logistical nightmares*. London: Routledge.

Shanghai Municipal Administration of Culture, Radio, Film, and TV [上海是文化廣播影視管理局]. (2012a). *Supportive and incentive measure of Shanghai animation and game industry (2012 Edition)* [上海動漫遊戲產業發展扶持獎勵辦法（2012年版）]. Retrieved from http://wenku.baidu.com/view/1714517e27284b73f2425045.html.

Shanghai Municipal Administration of Culture, Radio, Film & TV [上海是文化廣播影視管理局]. (2012b). Announcement of the release of supportive and incentive measures for the Shanghai animation and game industry (2012 Edition) [關於公佈《上海動漫遊戲產業發展扶持獎勵辦法（2012年版）的通知]. Retrieved from http://wgj.sh.gov.cn/wgj/node743/node912/node913/userobject1ai81063.html.

Simmie, J., & Sennett, J. (1999). Innovative clusters: Global or local linkages? *National Institute Economic Review, 170*, 87–98.

Sina Corporation. (2004a). The first education online game for minors Xue Lei Feng is launched. *People's Daily*. Retrieved from http://games.sina.com.cn/newgames/2004/06/060323081.shtml.

Sina Corporation. (2004b). [國內首款青少年教育網絡遊戲《學雷鋒》面世. 人民日報]. Retrieved from http://games.sina.com.cn/newgames/2004/06/060323081.shtml .

Shore, C., & Wright, S. (2003). *Anthropology of policy: Perspectives on governance and power*. London: Routledge.

SISPARK. (2008). Opinions of the Suzhou Municipal Government on supporting animation industries, and opinions of the Suzhou Industrial Park on promoting the original animation and game industry [蘇州工業園區關於推進原創動漫、遊戲產業發展的意見]. Retrieved from http://sme.sipac.gov.cn/Policy/PolicyDetail.aspx?ContentID=6207.

SISPARK. (2014). About SISPARK. Retrieved from http://www.sispark.com.cn/english/us/article.aspx?id=100005485.

Song, H., & Zhang, Y. [宋合營 & 張燕.]. (2004). The rating system of online games is released. "Dangerous" online games will be submitted for examination [網絡遊戲分級標準公佈 "危險級"網游將提交審查. 京華時報]. *Beijing Times*. Retrieved from http://news.xinhuanet.com/it/2004-11/29/content_2271128.htm.

Suzhou Municipal Government [蘇州市人民政府]. (2005). Opinions on supporting the development of animation and game industries [蘇州市人民政府關於扶持動漫產業發展的政策意見]. Retrieved from http://testcnci.cnci.gov.cn/2006/5/16/law-0102110100-2193.shtml.

Tang, X. [唐心怡]. (2004). The green games recommendable regulation was published to conduct age rating on online games [綠色遊戲推薦標準]出台對網游分級]. Retrieved from http://news.xinhuanet.com/game/2004-11/15/content_2220485.htm.

Towse, R. (2013). *A handbook of cultural economics*. (2nd ed.). Cheltenham, UK: Edward Elgar.

Towse, R. (2014). *Advanced introduction to cultural economics*. Cheltenham, UK: Edward Elgar.

UNIDO. (2001). Development of clusters and networks of SMEs. Retrieved from http://www.unido.org/fileadmin/user_media/Services/PSD/Clusters_and_Networks/SMEbrochure_UNIDO.pdf.

Wan, K. [萬凱]. (2010). The bottleneck and opportunities of the development of online game industry in Hongzhou [杭州網絡遊戲產業發展的瓶頸與機遇]. *Hangzhou Science & Technology* [杭州科技], *5*, 45–47.

World Creative. (2017). Cultural times: The first global map of cultural and creative industries. Retrieved from http://www.worldcreative.org .

Xinhua News Agency. (2007). The website of anti-corruption online game Qing Lian Zhan Shi was closed fifteen days after launch [反腐網游《清廉戰士》網站開張半月後關閉]. Retrieved from http://news.xinhuanet.com/newscenter/2007-08/16/content_6539891.htm .

Xinhua News Agency. (2009a). Report of the work of the government of 2009. [2009年政府工作報告]. Retrieved from http://news.xinhuanet.com/misc/2009-03/14/content_11010350.htm.

Xinhua News Agency. (2009b). The Ministry of Culture released 2009 white paper on the Chinese online game market [文化部發布《2009年中國網絡遊戲市場白皮書]. Retrieved from http://big5.gov.cn/gate/big5/www.gov.cn/jrzg/2010-01/18/content_1513701.htm.

Yazhou Zhoukan. (2014). *中國電子遊戲玩出政治. 亞洲週刊, 28*(5). Retrieved from http://www.yzzk.com/cfm/content_archive.cfm?id=1390449695448&docissue=2014-05&utm_source=twitterfeed&utm_medium=twitter.

YXdown.com. (2017). The classification scheme of online games passes the examination [網絡遊戲分級標準通過審核]. Retrieved from http://www.yxdown.com/news/24448.html.

Zacarelli, S. B. (2004). *Estratégia e sucesso nas empresas*. (4th ed.). São Paulo: Saraiva.

Zhang, H. [張寒]. (2010). Ministry of Culture responded to the proposal regarding shutting down Internet cafe. *Beijing News* [文化部回應網吧提案. 新京報]. Retrieved from http://finance.people.com.cn/GB/11079920.html.

Chapter Five

East Asian Cultural Policies and the Game Market

In the previous chapters, I reviewed China's cultural policy, demonstrating that it is based on a top-down model that is led by the ideology of the state. Thus the game ecology in China is constructed by the state, and most game companies survive financially, or are allowed to survive, based on economic logic. In other words, it is a political version of cultural policy that twists and in most cases speeds up the marketing and the consumption of games.

Venturing beyond the confines of government undertakings, this chapter examines how two East Asian competitors, South Korea and Japan, frame their cultural policies, mainly in the creative industries, and particularly in relation to game industries that are based on an economic model and a culturalist model. This chapter will examine the government actions and inactions that affect the development of a game industry in particular and the cultural and creative industries in general. Several policy instruments will be examined in the fields of economics, law, and education that affect the development of the game industry in South Korea and Japan. Moreover, the roles of the private sector, quasi-governmental organizations, and civic organizations that affect the ecosystem of the game industry and related creative industries are examined. The ways in which these East Asian competitors prepare (or remain unprepared) to compete with neighboring countries in terms of market growth and exports are considered. Based on government documents and secondary materials, the data from South Korea are supplemented by interviews with the Korea Creative Content Agency (KOCCA) and both major and minor game companies (e.g., NC Soft) that have been lured into this regional competition. The data on Japan's game industry were collected from research reports written by Mirko Ernkvist for the project "Mapping the Hong Kong Game Industry," for which I am the principal investigator. Subsequently, with the aim of an implicitly comparative cultural policy (Kawashima, 1995), an improved comprehensive cultural policy for Hong Kong is described in the final chapter.

CULTURAL POLICY IN SOUTH KOREA

The cultural policy of South Korea, as I have argued, is based on an economic approach in which control of content, the security of the state, and the ideologies concerned are not mentioned. Instead, South Korea's cultural policy is aimed at increasing the number of game sales, exports, and consumers, which are assessed largely based on economic growth. The positive outcomes of South Korea's state policies, as evidenced by the South Korean government in nurturing its game industry and other content industries, demonstrate the outcomes of this country's cultural policy. In 2014, an industry outlook report released by the Ministry of Culture, Sports, and Tourism and the KOCCA stated that the revenues of South Korea's content industry had reached 97.9 trillion won (US$91.1 billion), and exports amounted to US$5.75 billion (BusinessKorea, 2014). In the content industries, the game industry is the most prominent at 12.1 trillion won (US$11.25 billion). This amount was expected to expand, and the future shift from online games to mobile games was expected to foster huge growth (BusinessKorea, 2014). The case of South Korea is an example of or prototype for cultural policy in a democratic country.

The political economy of South Korea drives its growth. The fact that the nation's economy was largely agriculture-based with a per capita GDP of just US$67 in 1953 contrasts with its current economic success in general and its development of sophisticated content industries in particular (Chen, 2016). The year 1996 marked a milestone in South Korea's economic development as one of the fastest growing late-industrializing countries when it became a member of the Organization for Economic Cooperation and Development (Organization for Economic Cooperation and Development [OECD], 1996). In response to economic hardship caused by the 1997 Asian financial crisis, the South Korean government decided to transform the nation's economy by emphasizing innovation and creativity. The turning point was probably during the tenure of President Kim Dae-Jung (1998–2003), who heavily invested in infrastructure for digitalization in South Korea and introduced measures to promote the creative industries, including TV dramas, music, online games, and movies (Kwon & Kim, 2014). This era was followed by President Roh Moo-Hyun's government, which focused on information and communication technology (ICT) and cultural industries as engines of economic development (Kwon & Kim, 2014).

To support the development of the content industries, the South Korean government established KOCCA in May 2009. KOCCA is an umbrella agency, the composition of which is specified in Article 31 of the Framework Act on Cultural Industry Promotion. It combines the work of the South Korean Broadcasting Institute, the South Korean Culture and Content Agency, the South Korean Game Industry Agency, the Cultural Content Center, the Digital Content Business Group of South Korea, and the IT Industry Promotion Agency. KOCCA endeavors to "proactively respond to the convergence environment and focus on developing carefully selected killer content to lead the global content market" (Korea Creative Content Agency, 2017). As an agency dedicated to the promotion of all areas of content, KOCCA provides a comprehensive support system that aims at developing "the world's top 5 content powerhouses" in South Korea (Korea Creative Content Agency, 2017). The support system includes human resource development for the content industries; cultural technology development, which ranges from technology design, and production to content commercialization; and overseas market expansion. It also involves projects in digital broadcasting, game distribution promotion, and the digitalization of cultural contents. In my interview with KOCCA, their analysts clearly stated that this statutory body does not work alone but with representatives of the entire game industry in order to sharpen the competitiveness of the game industry. In addition to government initiatives to support the industry, the latter also asks KOCCA to lobby the government to support the industry. Compared to China's top-down model, KOCCA is based on an interactive model in which both the state and the industries cocreate cultural policy. It breaks away from the tradition that policies and laws are used by a government to control, regulate, and promote industries that are subservient to the state while the industries are bestowed with the economic benefit. In the context of South Korea, industry and government are united and cooperative, at least in the domain of the game industry, and they are symbiotic in the ecology of the creative industries.

The support of a comprehensive and steadfast government policy has played a major role in the international ascendance of the South Korean game industry. In Asia, industrial rivalry is usually predominant, with the exception of China. Thus the success of the South Korean game industry has not depended on surmounting Chinese competition but on its consistent policy of sustaining the domestic development of its game industry. It is fair to say that the South Korean government has played a decisive role in helping the local game industries gain momentum, whereby some games have become an international success. The year 1997 marked a watershed year for the South Korean game industry. In January 1997, the South Korean government announced a scheme to boost local game industries, which included the establishment of the South Korean Game Promotion Center (KGPC). This

measure not only placed the development of the South Korean game industries on the policy agenda but also set in motion a series of related state
initiatives. Until this point, the game industries scene in South Korea was
dominated by imported products from the U.S. and European markets. In
1998, the development of the game industries was officially included in the
development of the cultural industries. This move elevated the status of the
game industries beyond entertainment to become part of the national cultural
arena. The move also exemplified the South Korean government's foresight
in understanding the pervasiveness of game industries in the international
cultural market. The launch of the KGPC in July 1999 and its branch in Japan
two months later marked another major step in the government's plan to
nurture its local game industries. The KGPC's mission was to provide the
industry with necessary technological innovation and support, overseas market information, and venue and facility construction. The KGPC served as a
strategic interface between the government and the game industry. Hence it
enabled the government to keep abreast of the market and to facilitate industry practitioners in obtaining necessary and timely technological and market
guidance.

The founding of the Ministry of Culture and Tourism (MCT) in 1998, and
the transfer of the cultural assets policy portfolio, including the game industries, to its jurisdiction, served to enhance the industry's status as a South
Korean cultural asset (Ministry of Culture, Sports, and Tourism, 2017). The
launching of Cyber South Korea 21 in 1999 accelerated the game industry,
particularly the development of the online game industry, which included
broadband technology, thus rapidly increasing the number of Internet users
in South Korea and enhancing national Internet education about the positive
and negative aspects of cyber development. Moreover, the launch of KOC-
CA in the same year also boosted the South Korean game industry. Electronic games were among the content industries that were supported by KOCCA,
which also supported manga, animation, and music. KOCCA provided the
identified industries with support that covered equipment rental, investment,
technological training, international marketing strategies, advice, research on
medium- and long-term development, and strategic partnerships with overseas buyers and suppliers. To nurture talent in the booming game industries,
the South Korean government established the Game Academy in November
2000. A game investment association and a game investment valuation association were also established in December 2000 and June 2001, respectively,
to nurture talent and venture funding and investments to meet the needs of
the rising game industries (Chen, Y. W., 2011).

After two and a half years of operation, the KGPC was transformed into
the South Korean Game Industry Agency (KGIC). According to a white
paper released by the KGIC in April 2002, the booming game industries were
faced with a serious lack of both talent and money as well as a growing

difficulty in conquering the massive Chinese market. Many measures were taken, which are not reported in detail here. Finally, because of domestic limitations and failure in the competitive Asian market, the global market seemed a possible way of boosting the game industry. However, many of the global operations outside South Korea could no longer rely on its support.

Similar to its competitor China, South Korea also subscribes to the concept of cultural clusters. Seoul is in fact the largest cluster because all the major game companies with well-built Internet infrastructure are located in this city. Seoul has almost half of the population of South Korea, and it accounts for 48.2 percent of the GDP of the country (South Korean Statistical Information Service, 2017). In general, because the game industry is highly concentrated in Seoul, academics and policy makers in that city more or less decided that the clustering of various creative industries would enhance the coevolution of the industries (Berg, 2015). In particular, online game clusters are regarded as located at the intersection of ICT clusters and other creative industry clusters (Aruede et al., 2006, p. 14). The game clusters in Seoul function as value chains in which upstream firms are involved in computer graphic production, software development, and broadband Internet services, and downstream firms serve the users in online game cafes and other game media (Aruede et al., 2006, p. 15).

In addition, Seoul also designates certain areas for the location of high-tech corporations. The most prominent is Digital Media City, which is a high-tech complex for digital technology and the creative industries that was built in 2002. KOCCA and game development companies are also located in Digital Media City. However, differently from China, where local governmental cultural clusters offer many financial and other aids for game development, the Seoul version is a hub for creative industries where other state support is channeled through KOCCA and other government game agencies. In addition to the clusters in Seoul, South Korea has developed the city of Daejeon to the south of Seoul in order to develop an Asian version of Silicon Valley, where it accommodates eighteen universities, which mainly specialize in high-tech development. The development of mobile apps and game development takes place in Daejeon (Appsout, 2017) where the Daejeon Global Game Center was founded to specialize in developing games based on virtual reality (VR) and augmented reality (AR; Daejeon Metropolitan City, 2017).

Following online games, games with VR and AR features could be another area of competition between South Korea and China. The number of VR games created in China are few although investments of RMB¥6.82 billion were made in 2016 (GameRes, 2017), Tencent, the largest game company in China, listed the top VR game companies in 2015, which included Time of Virtual Reality, Baofeng Technology, VR Fires, Ruiyue Technology, 3Glasses, and ANTVR. However, only a few projects are actually on VR game platforms. In 2014, Time of Virtual Reality produced *Jiawu Reappearance*, which is a demo VR game animation of the Sino-Japanese War. In 2015, the VR game *Finding VR* was available on OcclusGearVR, a platform for VR games. There were 300,000 downloads on the Samsung Galaxy. However, VR games that are big hits both domestically and globally are yet to appear (Sina Games, 2016). AR games such as Pokémon Go involve location mapping, which inevitably intrudes on military spaces that are sensitive in the PRC. Thus, this AR game is not likely to appear in China. South Korea appears to be taking advantage of its free market to promote VR and AR games to compete globally. In 2017, a South Korean mobile game developer, YJM Games, jump-started the US$50 million Venture Reality Fund to finance VR, AR, and mixed reality start-ups (Takahashi, 2017). In 2016, the Ministry of Science, ICT, and Future Planning also inaugurated VR Flagship by investing US$158 million for three years in VR-related technology (Cho, 2016). At this time, although neither country has demonstrated considerable results, the unrestricted use of technology in South Korea seems to have created a favorable business environment.

Although South Korea is aware of the advantages of gaming and other Internet-related industries, it has always been cautious of cyber dysfunction. In 1999, it launched Cyber South Korea 21, a three-year Internet-PC project that was aimed at popularizing Internet access using affordable and efficient multimedia PCs (Telecompaper, 1999). There was a dual emphasis on cyber education and the prevention of dysfunctional consequences such as cyber-crime, Internet addiction, and access to violent and sexual content by under-age users. The policy regime governing the South Korean VR game world is very strict. A so-called identification policy requires that all players of South Korean–registered online games be identified by providing their personal identification number (as it appears on their identification card) and a personal computer registration number. The marketing identification number and personal identification number have to be included when players apply for a promotion account online. In other words, the governing authority requires that both users and service providers that register for online game use or provision in the South Korean VR game world are traceable. In principle, the authentic identity of users is not made known to other players, although service providers and the governing authorities have this information. The identification policy does not apply to online games registered in the international domain unless the game was originally imported from South Korea. The policy also does not apply to social media such as Facebook.

Another powerful regulatory policy is a so-called selective shutdown system. When a game is rated as requiring an excessive amount of playing time by young people, the South Korean government considers "shutting it down" for young users. For example, shooting games can only be played by people nineteen or older, and secondary school students are prohibited to play or buy the game *Diablo*. The government also forbids those under eighteen to play online games after midnight. Borrowing an adult's identity to play such online games is therefore a commonplace practice.

Unlike China, South Korea has a game classification system. The categorization is conducted by a game classification association that is empowered by law. Because of the presence and growing prominence of organizations such as Pan European Game Information (PEGI), the Entertainment Software Rating Board (ESRB), and game classification committees whose members are usually elected from civic groups, the game industry, academia, and youth groups, the government will likely reduce its direct role in game classification. This power may be transferred to industry groups such as PEGI and ESRB, as well as to game classification committees, in the near future.

As conceived by the Korea Game Development and Promotion Institute (KGDPI), the development of the South Korean game industry can be described by three stages: an importation stage (1980s), an import-substitution stage (1990s), and an ascendance stage (2000–Present). Before the 1990s, as expected, the game scene was dominated by American games, and there was no local production until 1994 when Samsung produced *Jurassic Park*, which has multiple-user dialog (MUD) (Game2, 2011). In 1996, MUD games were integrated with multiple-user graphic (MUG) games when Nexon launched the game *Empire of the Wind*, which two months later was followed by the release of *Gate of Hero* by Taewool. The latter became an early prototype of for South Korean online games. In September 1998, a mature type of online game was introduced with NC Soft's *Lineage*, a medieval fantasy MMORPG allowing ten thousand users to play at the same time, which completely replaced MUD and MUG games (Game2, 2011). The simplified gameplay of *Lineage* can be understood as a classic heroic story in which the player assumes the role of a knight (or other character) to form alliances in order to lay siege to a castle. NC Soft, which first released this game in the United States, was later publicly listed on Korean Securities Dealers Automated Quotations (KOSDAQ), a trading board of the Korean Exchange, which was a milestone for the game industry in South Korea. By 2000, there were sixty-one game companies in South Korea. The phenomenon of East Asian rivalry became apparent after 2000 when South Korean game industries sought to enter the Chinese market. In 2001, *Lineage II*—which was exported by South Korea's Wemade, produced by South Korea's Actoz Soft, and locally published by China's Shanda—became the first case of a "South Korean invasion of China" in terms of online games. At the apex of the game's popularity, the number of concurrent online players in China of *Lineage II* was 500,000 (Game2, 2011).

However, this "invasion" soon dissipated because of various factors in China. First, as we discussed in chapter 4, by 2000 China had developed a cultural policy to encourage its domestic companies to develop games, and the censorship of content was becoming increasingly formalized. After *Lineage II*, the influence of South Korean games diminished. Second, the local publisher of *Lineage II*, Shanda, published the online game *Lineage World*, which was accused of infringing the copyright of Wemade. The case was settled by both parties in 2007. This case demonstrates that in China, where the right of intellectual property is not respected, competition does not take place on a level playing field. The intellectual property holder, in this case the Korean company Wemade, was inevitably on the losing side.

In 2002, there was another wave of games exported from South Korea. The MMORPG *Ragnarok Online*, a game primarily based on Scandinavian legends but integrated with legends from Asia, Europe, and Africa was developed by the South Korean company Gravity. This game was successfully exported to more than fifty countries, including China, Taiwan, Japan, the United States, and Europe. A critical point was the fee required to play the game, which soon became an obstacle for its expansion in China and Taiwan, where free online games were the trend. In addition to its nontransactional nature—that is, the game did not encourage monetary transfer—this "pure" game failed to please audiences in China and Taiwan. Local operators in China and Taiwan also established free servers (which made the game free for users). Moreover, real money trade (RMT), *waigua*, and "gold farming" (i.e., a substitute player who helps another player who pays them to raise the game level of their character) became common. This phenomenon suggests that the cultural characteristics of a market can be a strong determinant of successful competition in the game industry. Then in 2003, the global popularity, including in South Korea, of the United State's MMORPG *World of Warcraft* heavily affected the local industry, and the South Korean game industry experienced its first crisis.

In 2005, Joogsik Woo, chairman of the board of the KGDPI proposed that the future strategy of the South Korean game industry should rely on global cooperation. Asian rivalry might be only a part of the globalization process. At that time, the East Asian market held 40 percent of the global world market. However, because China was on the rise and the influence of South Korean games was subsiding, South Korean games began to explore markets outside Asia. Since then, more than fifty South Korean games have been exported to thirty-five countries.

In 2006, because of South Korea's well-equipped technological infrastructure and its gaming technology, KOCCA in Japan, which possessed abundant intellectual property rights, sought to cooperate with South Korea in producing games. Games such as *SD World of Sword*, *Dragon Ball*, and *YS* were produced by the South Korean company CJ with Japanese storylines. CJ later produced the completely new Japanese online games *Unchartered Water* and *Dynasty Warrior Blast*. In the same year, South Korean game company Neowiz helped the United States' biggest game company, EA, operate the FIFA online game series, which was once poorly received in the market. Later EA and Neowiz established an alliance for game development, which was followed by greater international cooperation.

The lessons learned from the global cooperation of South Korea's game industry have strong implications for East Asian rivalry, in which China has always been the main competitor of Japan and South Korea. However, the competition on the terrain of popular culture and creative industries is now obvious. Although there was an embargo on Japanese popular cultural products in South Korea, now the import of audiovisual products is restricted in China. Each nation aims at exporting its cultural goods to the other nations. Such cutthroat competition, including cultural exports with tax rebates in South Korea and China, skews the market process. The present tendencies of the South Korean and Chinese game industries to globalize might help mitigate this regional competition, which is perhaps unhealthy and vicious.

CULTURAL POLICY IN JAPAN

In contrast to the case of South Korea, the long success of the Japanese game industry in mainly console video games has depended on free market supply and demand rather than on deliberate efforts by the government. From the early stages of the development of Japan's game industry to its worldwide prevalence (i.e., prior to 2000) there was no official or academic discussion of Japan's cultural policy. Cultural policy as a concept and discourse was considered in Japan at a much later phase, and it had less influence. In the following discussion, I will analyze the discourse of cultural policy based on the concept of "Cool Japan," which is associated with the global consumption of fashionable and chic Japanese cultural goods. This concept evolved into the Cool Japan Fund, which supports projects that propagate and praise both traditional and contemporary Japanese culture. Therefore, the case of the Japanese cultural industry can be conceived as tending toward a culturalist perspective. In addition, specific measures target the game industries, but the main lesson that Japan's cultural policy addresses is the social good. Microlevel regulations help Japan's mature and thriving game industry grow healthily and sustainably while minimizing the harm caused by game addiction and virtual crimes. Hence, Japanese cultural policy is not driven by profit, and it is often motivated by sociological considerations.

Japan has a short history of cultural policy making, but this does not mean that it has no policy regarding the creative industries. Around 2002, the concept Cool Japan was adopted by the Japanese government as a strategy for promoting Japan's creative industries. At that time, the term "Gross National Cool" was used to refer to Japan's revival as a cultural superpower, a revival equivalent to the globalizing effects of culture (McGray, 2002). In 2012, Japan's creative industries accounted for 2 trillion yen in the global market, which was estimated to reach 900 trillion yen in 2020. The Ministry of Economy, Trade and Industry (METI) is responsible for promoting Japan's creative industries both domestically and overseas based on the concept of Cool Japan (Nagata, 2012). For example, in 2011, METI sponsored thirteen projects in eight countries, including China and South Korea (Nagata, 2012). In 2012, the Creative Industries Promotion Office was established by METI to promote Japan's creative industries under Cool Japan. However, as a government initiative to promote Japanese cultural products, Cool Japan mainly includes J-pop; animation; film; design; fashion; and Japanese *kwaii*, or cute icons, such as Hello Kitty, Little Twin Stars, Dodoro, and most recently, Pokémon. Games are rarely included in this promotion. When the Cool Japan Fund was founded in 2013 as a public-private fund for supporting and promoting "the development of demand overseas for excellent Japanese products and services," on its official website, the game industry was not mentioned. The projects funded are not aimed at strengthening the financial basis of the industries concerned. In fact, much of the funding sponsors single events and activities or those lasting for a short period on the condition that these cultural texts and cultural phenomenon are publically marketed, represented, and manifested to promote Japanese culture. At this time, the Cool Japan Fund has not yet aided a project in the game industry.

In Japan, no ministry-level governance exists to oversee the game industry, and addiction to online gaming in Japan has been widely reported by the media. A nineteen-year-old male player was widely reported to spend 80 percent of his allowance on gaming monthly (Kay, 2012). The report suggested control of gaming rather than a subsidizing mentality should be applied to gaming. Concrete guidelines for the protection of gamers are therefore produced by some agencies. A Consumer Affairs Agency (CAA) was established in 2009. In 2012, its mandate was extended to include the protection of consumer rights related to trade, labeling, and safety, which seemingly targeted competitors (*Japan Times*, 2009; Consumer Affairs Agency, 2017). However, subsequently jurisdiction was expanded to the game industry when free-to-play models indirectly desensitized player-consumers' cost awareness because they spent more money on virtual goods in the games (Lin & Sun, 2011). A major concern was the popular game *Complete Gacha* (*Kompu Gacha*), in which players are offered a prize or a valuable virtual item in the online game after they purchase a certain type of item (NeoGAF, 2012). The CAA regarded this game as a form of gambling and began to investigate improper sale methods on major social networking services (SNS) sites in response to complaints that game companies charged players exorbitant fees on sites such as Gree and Mobage (NeoGAF, 2012).

Triggered by the phenomenon of *Complete Gacha*, the Japanese Social Game Association called for self-regulation and control of the industry. Previously, six game companies, Gree, DeNA, Mixi, CyberAgency, Dwango, and LINE operation NHN, had established a council to devise measures for self-regulation (Toto, 2012). Their efforts included taking major countermeasures against RMT, imposing payment caps on players under the age of eighteen, clarifying game rules and explanations, establishing working groups, and promoting closer ties among relevant organizations (Ernkvist, 2014). Moreover, in response to a demand by the Ministry of Internal Affairs and Communications, the Content Evaluation and Monitoring Association (EMA), an independent and self-regulatory organization, was established in 2008. The EMA offers mobile-content examination services, monitors the effects of websites, certifies safe websites, and oversees services that prevent children and youth from accessing mobile websites that contain materials unsuitable for their consumption (Content Evaluation and Monitoring Association, 2017). Many online game companies use the EMA's evaluation of game content to prove that their game content is appropriate for adolescents (Ernkvist, 2014).

In Japan, advertising that promotes online gaming is always an issue. Although online games are advertised as "free games," gamers cannot enjoy the full experience of gaming if they cannot afford to pay for the extra devices, tools, and items advertised in each game (Hara & Nakagawa, 2011). Presumably, this advertising promotes these free online games but fails to provide sufficient information to gamers, particularly young consumers and children, regarding the games' inherent costs. Consequently, the CAA has requested that sufficient information be provided to players in this type of advertising (Hara & Nakagawa, 2011).

Another game-related industry association, the Japanese Online Game Association (JOGA), has also launched various measures for the self-regulation of the game industry, measures ranging from promoting safety and security guidelines to encouraging members to follow the regulations of the Premiums and Representation Act implemented by the CAA as well as tax laws that apply to online gaming. In addition, JOGA arranges business matching for its members, and it conducts annual research on the game industry (Japanese Online Game Association, 2017).

With regard to the persistent question of RMT, all virtual currency on SNS platforms and in social games is regulated by legislation such as the Act on the Settlement of Funds (e.g., Order for Enforcement of the Act on Settlement of Funds, Cabinet Office Ordinance, and on Prepaid Payment Instruments, and Cabinet Office Ordinance on Fund Transfer Service Providers). The RMT of game items and currencies is somewhat controversial (Lehdonvirta & Ernkvist, 2011). RMT is useful for players who prefer to buy time and enhance their odds of winning a game. In certain Japanese social games, buying rare virtual cards from other players can even help a player save money (Ernkvist, 2014). Despite joint efforts by SNS platform holders, RMT is still widespread, particularly on some famous online auction sites. To further regulate RMT and *Complete Gacha*, Ernkvist (2014) proposed that the Japanese government consider allowing the Financial Instruments and Exchange Law (originally the Securities and Exchange Law) regulate the game market.

Thus in Japan, different administrative measures are applied to the game industry. Such measures are mainly aimed at regulating the game industry to prevent it from causing social harm to players, particularly minors and children. An examination of these regulatory measures reveals that compared to South Korea and China, online games in Japan are not considered driving forces of the economy. Instead, they are viewed as possibly undesirable forms of entertainment that are tolerated by society. Thus, cultural policy is made using a sociological approach instead of a political-economic approach. As I suggested at the beginning of this section, the Japanese game industry is largely a self-made success, and it has little formal regulatory rapport with or concrete financial support from the government. Not until 2006 did the Japanese government provide "help" to the video game industry by offering various strategies to the industry (Ministry of Economy Trade and Industry, 2006), and the support was very minimal.

In this regard, the findings of any study of cultural policy vis-à-vis the Japanese game industry will differ greatly from the findings of studies of cultural policy in Japan at large. In general, studies of Japanese cultural policy in the postwar period have concluded that because of unstable geopolitics in neighboring territories, Japanese authorities chose to exercise a cultural diplomacy that supported the export of Japanese pop culture and lifestyles in order to achieve a certain kind of soft power (Otmazgin, 2012). The popularity and familiarity of Japanese culture means that the people of China and South Korea accept Japanese culture and that there has been an attenuation of the hatred engendered by Japan's invasion of China and South Korea in World War II. However, because game exportation is not explicitly included in the Cool Japan project, it is reasonable to argue that games and the game industry in Japan are not overtly included in its cultural diplomacy. To a certain extent, my argument is consistent with that of Iwabuchi (2015), who claimed that a very limited diversity of culture was used by Japan in its pop-culture diplomacy, and that this diplomacy was not aimed at a mutual, cross-cultural dialogue. In this case, despite the prevalence of Japanese games worldwide, they are not emphasized as much as Hello Kitty is in Japanese communication overseas. Such games have the potential to be the interface through which cross-cultural understanding can be enhanced.

China's cultural clusters and South Korea's cultural clusters represent governmental top-down strategies for promoting the creative industries and increasing competitive power. In Japan, however, such clusters do not exist. Although game companies may collaborate to achieve competitive advantages, this clustering is based solely on the business decisions of the game companies. Based on an analysis of a database of social game companies, Ernkvist (2014) found that 79 percent of social game companies of Japan were heavily concentrated within the Tokyo metropolitan area, particularly in the Shinjuku, Shibuya, Minato, and Chiyoda wards. Ernkvist (2014) found that clustering first occurred in the historical formation of brands in areas such as Akihabara and Kanda in the Chiyoda and Shinjuku wards, which are hubs of video game companies. These wards offer convenient transportation and an abundant supply of talent from universities in the area. In a study of the geocultural locations of console video game companies, Hanzawa and Yamamoto (2017) found that urban and industrial agglomeration led to a redundancy of constituent firms—a clustering effect that enhanced creativity instead of efficiency.

Japan has led the world in the console video games produced by Sony and Nintendo. Sony established Sony Interactive Entertainment in 1994 to launch its original video game console, PlayStation. Sony's best-selling console game, PlayStation 2, which was released in 2000, has sold more than 155 million units. Nintendo developed into a video game company in the 1970s and developed Pokémon Go with AR technology in 2016. In 2004, an unprecedented 154 million units of the console Nintendo DS were sold.

Recently, Sony and Nintendo have developed online distribution platforms by which games can be downloaded and purchased. Similar to iOS and Android, which have become the most common platforms for mobile games, Sony's and Nintendo's online platforms for their own self-published games, *PlayStation Network* and *Wii Ware*, compete with Microsoft's *Xbox Live Arcade* (Bogost, Ferrari, & Schweizer, 2010). These platforms allow the game developers to self-publish games, all royalties accruing to the platform developer. The flexible pricing strategies of Japanese platforms have enabled them to outsell Xbox (French, 2008).

With regard to online games, which are the focus of this book, popular Japanese games have prevailed in Asia, particularly those published in China for the mass Chinese market. These online games include *Cross Gate*, *Lineage*, *Monster Hunter*, and *Phantasy Star Online Blue Blast*. In Japan, KOEI is a leading online game corporation and responsible for *Unchartered Water Online*, *Nobunaga's Ambition Online*, and *Sangokushi Online*, which have been published in different Asian markets. Unlike China and South Korea, where the state imposes measures to empower private commercial game corporations in regional competition, the popularity of Japanese games is due to cooperation with local publishers.

As far as the game industry is concerned, Japanese authorities do not focus on a rivalry with East Asian countries and China. With the exception of token support, very few governmental measures have been implemented to sponsor or to promote the game industry in Japan. No industry voices have been raised to "win back" cultural territory in online gaming that has been occupied largely by Chinese and South Korean corporations. Instead, Japanese game companies such as Nintendo and Sony focus on exporting console video games to international markets. Strategies for a competitive, regional, online game market are largely nonexistent.

THE POLICY VACUUM IN HONG KONG'S CREATIVE INDUSTRIES

The East Asia cultural policies examined in this chapter have a simple implication for Hong Kong. Compared to the complicated and varied cultural policies of China, multilevel support in South Korea, and the Cool Japan initiative, Hong Kong has yet to react to regional "efforts" and competition. In a nutshell, the public perception is that the HKSAR government is slow and reluctant to react. The state-driven cultural economy of the countries surrounding Hong Kong are in stark contrast to Hong Kong's laissez-faire approach. In Hong Kong, there are no policies, regulations, or laws regarding the creative industries. There are no guidelines or regulations for the game industry or proactive strategies for the promotion, financial support, and development of this industry. Because Hong Kong is a city without any support from the state, in reality, it is not feasible for Hong Kong's game industry to compete with its Asian competitors when those competitors are each supported by their country's government.

The longer Hong Kong waits, the higher the aspiration that Hong Kong should learn from its neighbors. The Chinese case and the South Korean case are relevant to the HKSAR because the public believe that a state-led model of game industry development has proven to be a strong economic driver almost across the board. Japan's cultural industries which used to be prevalent in Hong Kong in general follows a market-led model, and it is one balanced with the principle of social good. However, this model is not included in the current discourse in the Hong Kong community. As a matter of fact, the current discourse of cultural policy in Hong Kong preclude the social or moral dimension of it. Suffice it to say, the Hong Kong public is generally not aware of Japan's cultural policy or Cool Japan, which does not offer events and activities in Hong Kong. On the contrary, South Korean TV dramas, variety shows, and games (online games such as *Lineage II* in 2003, *Talesrunner* in 2005, and *Audition Online* in 2006 as well as mobile games such as *Lineage II: Revolution* in 2016 and *Talesrunner Revolt* in 2017) are daily popular culture consumed in Hong Kong. The popularity of these cultural products reinforces the public's impression and perhaps the government's perception that the South Korean model of cultural policy could effectively drive the South Korean creative industries. Then the logic is that Hong Kong should follow suit.

Moreover, after the Asian financial crisis, South Korea's speedy economic turnaround and the popularity of the "Korean Wave" (*hallyu*) over Hong Kong pop culture were evidence of the predominance of the South Korean model. It is believed that South Korea rebounded economically because of the success of its innovative industries, including the game industry. Hong Kong wants to imitate this model. Hong Kong's economy, which has often been criticized as being too heavily reliant on finance and property, has yet to determine an effective way to diversify. Nurturing the cultural industries, especially the game industry, seems to be a possible solution.

In strong contrast to the success stories in South Korea, where policy supports the cultural industries, the Hong Kong game industry has not seen government action. In fact, it could be said that in Hong Kong, the game industry is a non-category and a non-item on the government's policy agenda. There has been no mention of the game industry in the territory's Policy Address and Policy Agenda. No policy has been established or implemented to rate games or enhance game-related, virtual world governance, including the virtual currencies used for online transactions. Consequently, tax incentives, support for industrial research, and government efforts to attract international game companies are all absent in the HKSAR.

As we've seen, different levels of government activism and varied policy packages have been effective in game industry development. However, a common denominator for success is government involvement in its domestic game industry. From state-dictated production of games in China and the South Korean government's multilayered and comprehensive state policy of promoting its cultural industries to the Japanese government's passive role in regulating the virtual environment, countries with government involvement play a significant role in developing the game industry. Should Hong Kong wish to develop a more vibrant game scene or a much better-utilized economic driver propelled by the game industry in order to compete with its neighbors, the government must to a certain extent learn from existing models of game industry development. Hong Kong's game industry stands a good chance of winning the economic competition in the Asian region because of its strong links to international markets, well-connected global network, and high ability to produce Chinese-language games and products. Hong Kong's counterparts (i.e., South Korea, Japan, and China) all compete based on different degrees of governmental support. Therefore, the HKSAR government's strategic presence is required in the international global game scene. If Hong Kong continues to believe in yesterday's myth of a bottom-up, market-led industry developmental model, it will lag behind the content-based, knowledge-driven economies of the East Asian region.

REFERENCES

Appsout. (2017). Mobile apps and games development company in Daejeon, South Korea. Retrieved from http://www.appsout.com/global-sites/mobile-apps-game-development-company-daejeon-south-korea/.

Aruede, Nomyo, Cheng, Xiaopeng, Jurng, Chuljoong, Nguyen, . . . & Euna. (2006). Microeconomics of competitiveness: Republic of South Korea online game cluster. MOC Project. Retrieved from http://www.isc.hbs.edu/resources/courses/moc-course-at-harvard/Documents/pdf/student-projects/SouthKorea_Online_Game_Cluster_2006.pdf.

Berg, S. H. (2015). Creative cluster evolution: The case of film and TV industries in Seoul, South Korea. *European Planning Studies, 23*(10), 1993–2008.

Bogost, I., Ferrari, S., & Schweizer, B. (2010). *Newsgame: Journalist at play.* Boston: MIT Press.

BusinessKorea. (2014). Content industry in 2014: Sales of digital content industry estimated at 100 trillion wong this year. Retrieved from http://businesskorea.co.kr/english/news/money/3204-content-industry-2014-sales-digital-content-industry-estimated-100-trillion-won-year.

Chen, Q. (2016). From post-war ruin to "miracle of Han River": Why did South Korea rapidly develop? [從戰後廢墟到「漢江奇蹟」韓國為何迅速崛起？] *China Times.* Retrieved from http://hottopic.chinatimes.com/20160613003781-260812.

Chen, Y. W. (2011). Creative industries policy from the perspective of complex theory: A case study of how South Korea drives smart family. *Journal of Technology Management, 16*(4), 77–104. Retrieved from http://www.ta.tku.edu.tw/people/writing_journal.php?Sn=19.

Cho, J. Y. (2016). Room for experience: "Virtual reality bang" to open in South Korea next month. *BusinessKorea.* Retrieved from http://www.businesskorea.co.kr/english/news/ict/14640-room-vr-experience-'virtual-reality-bang'-open-korea-next-month.

Consumer Affairs Agency. (2017). Retrieved from http://www.caa.go.jp/en/.

Cool Japan Fund. (2017). What is Cool Japan Fund? Retrieved from https://www.cj-fund.co.jp/en/about/cjfund.html.

Content Evaluation and Monitoring Association. (2017). An introduction to the Content Evaluation and Monitoring Association (EMA). Retrieved from http://www.ema.or.jp/en/dl/introduction.pdf.

Daejeon Metropolitan City. (2017). Full operation of the Daejeon global game center for VR and AR game industry. Retrieved from http://daejeon.go.kr/dre/DreBoardNoticeView.do;jsessionid= geYhIzZF8y9BoHc4ZiQTBuvNTKlfM3voBwyeS4rFUaSkMWGugurFJcZu4ZVygbNT. WEB1_servlet_engine2?ntatcSeq=1084925847&boardId=normal_0133&menuSeq=2751&pageIndex=1.

Ernkvist, M. (2014). The Japanese social game industry 2013. Retrieved from http://creativeindustries.com.cuhk.edu.hk/wp-content/uploads/2014/12/Japanese-Game-Industry-Report-2013.pdf.

French, M. (2008). Nintendo's "secret war" on Xbox Live Arcade and PlayStation Store. Retrieved from http://www.develop-online.net/news/nintendo-s-secret-war-on-xbox-live-arcade-and-playstation-store/0102541.

Game2. (2011). South Korean online game history. Retrieved from http://blog.game2.tw/韓國網絡遊戲發展史 -.WTj511L3VZ0.

GameRes. (2017). China VR industry white paper: 2020 market becomes mature. [中国VR产业白皮书：2020年市场趋于成熟] *Sohu.* Retrieved from http://www.sohu.com/a/130049434_502377.

Hanzawa, S., & Yamamoto, D. (2017). Recasting the agglomeration benefits for innovation in a hit-based cultural industry: Evidence from the Japanese console videogame industry. *Geografiska Annaler: Series B, Human Geography, 99*(1), 59–78.

Hara, A., & Nakagawa, N. (2011). Advertising to children in Japan. *Young Consumers, 12*(4). Retrieved from http://www.emeraldinsight.com/doi/full/10.1108/yc.2011.32112daa.003.

Iwabuchi, K. (2015). Pop culture diplomacy in Japan: Soft power, nation branding and the question of "international cultural exchange." *International Journal of Cultural Policy, 21*(4), 419–432.

Japan Times. (2009). Consumer affairs agency bill ok'd. Retrieved from http://www. japantimes.co.jp/news/2009/04/17/news/consumer-affairs-agency-bills-okd/-. WTuoxlL3VZ0.

Japanese Online Game Association. (2017). Information. Retrieved from http://www. japanonlinegame.org.

Kang, H. (2015). Contemporary cultural diplomacy in South Korea: Explicit and implicit approaches. *International Journal of Cultural Policy, 21*(4), 433–447.

Kawashima, N. (1995). Comparative cultural policy: Towards the development of comparative study. *European Journal of Cultural Policy, 1*(2), 289–307.

Kay. (2012). Online gaming addiction becoming serious in Japan. Retrieved from https:// japantoday.com/category/features/lifestyle/online-game-addiction-becoming-serious-problem-in-japan.

Korea Creative Content Agency. (2017). KOCCA. Retrieved from http://www.kocca.kr/cop/ main.do.

Kwon, S. H., & Kim, J. (2014). The cultural industry policies of the South Korean government and the South Korean wave. *International Journal of Cultural Policy, 20*(4), 422–439.

Lehdonvirta, V., & Ernkvist, M. (2011). Converting the virtual economy into development potential: Knowledge map of the virtual economy. Washington, DC: InfoDev, World Bank.

Lin, H., & Sun, C. T. (2011). Cash trade in free-to-play online games. *Games and Culture, 6*(3), 270–287.

McGray, D. (2002). Japan's gross national cool. *Foreign Policy*. Retrieved from http://www. douglasmcgray.com/cool-japan.html.

Ministry of Culture, Sports and Tourism. (2017). History. Retrieved from http://www.mcst.go. kr/english/ministry/history/history3.jsp.

Ministry of Economy Trade and Industry. (2006). The direction of game industries strategies [Ｍ―ム産業戦略の策定に向けて] Retrieved from http://www.meti.go.jp/committee/ materials/downloadfiles/g60428c03j.pdf.

Nagata, K. (2012). Exporting culture via "cool Japan." *Japan Times*. Retrieved from http:// www.japantimes.co.jp/news/2012/05/15/reference/exporting-culture-via-cool-japan/-. WTufzlL3XGI.

NeoGAF. (2012). Japan *gatcha* system for games on SNS may be legally considered gambling. Retrieved from http://www.neogaf.com/forum/showthread.php?t=473025.

Organization for Economic Cooperation and Development (OECD). (1996). *The knowledge-based economy*. Paris: Organization for Economic Cooperation and Development.

Otmazgin, N. (2012). Geopolitics and soft power: Japan's cultural policy and cultural diploma-cy in Asia. *International Journal of Cultural Policy, 19*(1), 37–61.

Sina Games. (2016). Interview with Wang Shi Yuan: Taking space shuttle to go into VR world. [專訪TVR王世元：乘上時光機穿梭VR世界]. *Read01*. Retrieved from https://read01. com/ya8ayg.html-.WbEjf633VR0.

South Korean Statistical Information Service. (2017). Retrieved from http://kosis.kr/eng/.

Takahashi, D. (2017). South Korea's YJM Games invests in the VR Fund. *Venture Beat*. Retrieved from https://venturebeat.com/2017/01/17/south-koreas-yjm-games-invests-in-the-vr-fund/.

Telecompaper. (1999). Cyber South Korea 21 project launched. Retrieved from https://www. telecompaper.com/news/cyber-korea-21-project-launched-189760.

Toto, S. (2012). JASGA: Japan gets social game association. Retrieved from http://www. serkantoto.com/2012/11/09/jasga-japan-social-game-association-social-games/.

Woo, J. (2016). The strategies for future game industry & global cooperation. Retrieved from http://www.wcec-secretariat.org/en/pdf/08/woo_jongsik_16.pdf.

Chapter Six

Beyond the East Asian Rivalry and Hong Kong's Creative Industries

In this concluding chapter, I'll examine the relationships among the game market, the game industries, and the cultural policy of East Asian countries and regions. I'll also consider the thesis of East Asian rivalry, or the perceived competition in terms of soft power among East Asian countries. Because this book is about cultural policy, I would like to offer a paradigm of critical cultural policy that includes more than practices of cultural policy in other countries as potential models for Hong Kong. Instead, although policy recommendations could be made, I intend to propose a normative view of cultural policy in order to determine whether the recommendations offered by governments or inferred from models of cultural industries are beneficial for industries, citizens, and the social good.

DO WE NEED A CULTURAL POLICY FOR GAMING?

In a marketing survey of video game consumers in 2016, it was estimated that the number of gamers worldwide had reached 1.8 billion (Mygaming, 2016). In 2017, there were 2.2 billion gamers worldwide (Newzoo, 2017a). Gaming has become an indispensable part of the daily lives of billions of citizens across the globe. Gaming has been accepted as a new form of digital entertainment, a means of education, and as a profession in the realm of communication technology and devices. Given the ever-increasing number of consumers and professionals involved, it is no wonder that the game industry has developed into a mature creative domain. The scale of the global online game industry (US$99.6 billion in 2016; Newzoo, 2016) has already exceeded all the major creative industries, such as the film industry (US$38 billion in 2016; Statista, 2016), and it has far surpassed the music industry (US$15 billion in 2016; International Federation of the Phonographic Industry, 2016). However, in Hong Kong, despite demonstrated growth in previous years, a huge China market, the East Asian markets, and an increasing number of local users, the game industry has remained stagnant. In my interview with a representative of a major company in Hong Kong, the game industry was estimated to be US$120 million.

Thus, the discourse in the HKSAR and the game industry and in other creative industries includes the opinion that new processes, methods, and strategies are required to cope with the current stagnation. This book has examined this discourse, the market forces that influence it, and the cultural policies that both construct and are constructed by it. The fact that Hong Kong's creative industries have been co-opted by China and overwhelmed by the creative industries of South Korea led to the main thesis of the book: On the terrain of the game industry, there is a local discourse of Hong Kong's rivalry with East Asia. It is believed that through cultural policy, including government financial support, logistic enhancement, and the clustering effect, Hong Kong could acquire the soft power to regain a market that has been seized by its Asian competitors and even to dominate its counterparts in the game industry. In this book, however, I did not evaluate the validity of this discourse. In fact, in the cases of South Korea and China, the evidence indicates that the validity of the discourse might be indisputable. Based on data collected from surveys, policy reports, market reports, and interviews, the chapters in this book provide evidence of the reasons that this discourse in Asia has become legitimate, robust, and dogmatic. This last chapter, instead of offering a new policy solution or reiterating existing policy solutions to the position of Hong Kong's game industry, will provide a critical conclusion regarding possible directions for cultural policy designed for the game industry. The metanarratives in the discourse of cultural policy in the East Asian context will also be discussed. Finally, the potential political, social, and economic implications of a cultural policy for the creative industries in Hong Kong will be explicated.

DIVERSE MODELS OF CULTURAL POLICY

The first critical response to the state-driven East Asian rivalry is that it eliminates all possibility of the development of the creative industries. Under state-driven cultural policy, through ingenious forms of comics and animation as well as online and mobile games, the game industry developed at a fast pace in tandem with economic development and social betterment. Comprehensive and steadfast governmental support played a major role in the international ascendance of the South Korean game industry. Under the state's directive, China has replaced the United States as the largest game market in the world. However, so far, the fast development of the game industry in South Korea and China has occurred within the last thirty years and twenty years, respectively. In the 1980s, South Korea was still in the stage of importation, and in China, few games were developed domestically prior to 2000. The state-driven success of cultural policy in these countries doesn't prove that creativity can be sustained in the long term. Moreover, the creative industries developed by this model might not withstand competition in a free-market economy. Despite increasing exportation, none of the online games developed in China are prevalent in the world, and those exported overseas are played mainly by ethnic Chinese consumers. In South Korea, the most successful games, such as *Lineage II*, are popular mainly in Chinese communities in East Asia. Thus, whether state-driven cultural policy will be able to compete with market forces in the global market is still unknown.

In contrast to the cases of South Korea and China, the success of the Japanese game industry is mainly due to market forces instead of direct governmental support. Unlike China and South Korea, in Japan, the role of cultural policy is to offset any excessive commercial forces that accompany the practices of its gaming industry. The main lesson is that Japan's relevant cultural policies demonstrate that the regulatory and legal environment of Japanese society has helped its mature and thriving game industry grow healthily and sustainably while minimizing the harm caused directly or indirectly by game addiction and virtual crime. The case of Japan demonstrates that a cultural policy that drives gaming and boosts the industry is therefore largely without pitfalls, unintended consequences, or adverse social effects (Gray, 2009). However, in the mainstream discourse of cultural policy, the optimization and maximization of efficiency of industrial output always displace the negative discourse of the cultural industries. In the global discourse of the cultural industries, the Japanese model is clearly an alternative because it attempts to balance the economic benefits and detrimental effects of gaming in society. Nevertheless, it is too early to say that this model is superior to the state-driven model of cultural policy making applied by the Chinese and South Korean governments.

In a global context, the state-driven model is unique to East Asia and China; in addition, the philosophy, target, and means of support are different. In the EU, for example, the support provided to the cultural industries differs notably in its sophistication. It might be true that the methods are similar and that the common means are tax incentives, subsidies, industry classification, and regulations offered at the national level. However, based on Behrman's analysis (2011, p. 3), the EU initiative does not provide full-fledged support at all levels of development of the game industry for it is believed that such support would diminish the competitiveness of the game companies. In the EU, the state tends to support the start-up companies. Countries with sizable game industries, most notably France, Ireland, the UK, Finland, and the Netherlands, try to provide public finance to buttress local businesses (Nieborg and de Kloet, 2016).

Although competitive models were used to precipitate the East Asian market, alternative models are absent from the East Asian discourse. Contrary to the East Asian model, in Southeast Asia, the Association of Southeast Asian Nations (ASEAN) and the Asian Economic Community (AEC) serve as a central, inter-governmental bureau that has produced a pan–Southeast Asian strategy for promoting the game industry. With the AEC as its agent, Southeast Asia has attracted multinational game companies because of the access it offers to an abundant pool of skilled, English-speaking workers and a warm reception of the expertise and knowledge of Western game art and storytelling. In some instances, the location of these companies in the region is partly in response to incentives offered by individual governments. In other words, instead of competing, different Southeastern Asian states work together to expand their markets by serving as an Asian hub in which American game companies subcontract jobs (Fung, 2016).

Non-Asian countries might not forsake the state-directed model, but the evidence indicates that they are cautious about upsetting market logic. Thus in Australia, tax breaks are given to game companies through agencies such as the Department of Innovation, Industry, Science, and Research, the Australian government's trade and investment development agency, whereas federal and state governments focus on the research and development of funding schemes for technologies such as game engines.

In the North American game industry, at the federal level, Canada offers competitive corporate tax rates to game companies, and individual provinces focus on research. For example, some provinces offer refundable tax credits for the production of interactive digital media and scientific research and experimental development tax credits (Banks and Keane, n.d.). The United States provides tax incentives to game companies, and large portions of the industry are concentrated in California, Texas, Washington, New York, and Massachusetts. These companies at one time provided more than 22,000 jobs in the video game industry, which accounted for 71 percent of the video game industry in United States (Banks and Keane, n.d.).

Therefore, outside East Asia, diverse models of cultural policy exist that Hong Kong and other East Asian countries might adopt and follow. Even within China, different regional authorities have preferential policies that support the development of the game industry. Shanghai has a public service platform for the game industry to increase the efficiency of its supporting services and improve the investment environment, whereas Guangzhou emphasizes professional certification of game enterprises and regulation of the game market. Indeed, the current discourse of the cultural policy of creative industries is largely inclined to direct governmental support, which is equivalent to a state's financial support, which disrupts market logic and reduces the time required for development. This industrial push, as well as expectations of the public, not only disrupts market logic but also is a pretext for political manipulation of the economy. Hence the countries of Europe and North America are vigilant with regard to direct financial support of the game industry by their governments. However, this is not to say that a state-driven model is necessarily evil; successful cases of governmental support have resulted in the prosperity of South Korea and China. The diverse models of cultural policy considered in this book provide some of the much-needed information Hong Kong needs to make decisions and choose measures that will benefit Hong Kong society. These models also provide Asia with potent evidence that the dominant discourse of a state-driven model of cultural policy is not the only hegemonic model. I further argue that state directives could easily slip into state control of the industry and hence manipulation of the free market. In the long term, it could evolve into the state's dictation of consumers' taste—that is, their needs and wants would be prescribed by the state.

CULTURAL POLICY: THE PROBLEM OF COMMERCE OVER CONTENT

Is it true that cultural policy *in effect* benefits the social good? Cultural policy has evolved into a formal field of study in various disciplines such as cultural studies, media and communication studies, sociology, and anthropology. In these disciplines, cultural policy has become a metanarrative that dominates the circle of knowledge inquiry. Thus it is essential to use a critical and cultural studies approach if not to contest, then to balance the instrumental approach to cultural policy.

Although I do not deny the value of cultural policy in the development of the game industry, we should at least ask a fundamental question: What is the nature of the cultural texts that these game industries produce? Although the cultural policy of a nation may serve to construct "healthy" creative industries without consigning creative work to political control, this does not mean that it will generate content that is conducive to improvement of the community. The benchmark of the success of creative industries is their economic success, which is based on instrumental assessment. An effective business solution might increase the revenues of the creative industries but it will not necessarily produce social "values" (Gray, 2009) or creative content that will promote the betterment of society. When the success of the creative industries is defined by momentary revenue and returns, commercial interest takes precedence over cultural content.

In fact, our review of the cultural policies governing the game industry in China in chapter 4 showed that few state subsidies produced "good" game content. The only exception may be China's censorship system and its national "green" scheme that are aimed at censoring game content that contradicts state ideologies and agendas. Moreover, in the government's various five-year plans, the PRC has set commercial goals to expand and regulate the game industries in order to fund viable business plans and strategies. The state directives never consider whether game content should be creative.

Hence the Hong Kong government should be able to learn from China how best to establish an effective institution that actively underwrites game development based on the same commercial logic. Assuming that no political interest is involved, the projects funded will deliver commercial promise in a neoliberal economy—not creative games that embed values beneficial to Hong Kong. We might then ask the following questions: What is a creative game? And what is a game with good values? There are no immediate answers. Nonetheless, I am sure that constant social innovation, perceivable economic affluence, and relatively individual autonomy will dovetail impeccably in an ideal social development and that in such a society, games can be the social driver. In this era of global capitalism, the incentive for innovators to aim for this goal is straightforwardly commercial, and such innovation can be driven by the cultural policy of the state.

HONG KONG'S CHOICE

In the four areas considered in this book, there is a strong tendency toward the commercial domination of cultural policy. However, we have also seen that these are diverse models of cultural policy, some of which might generate a more balanced outcome. For instance, the Cool Japan fund champions projects that promote Japanese culture, and their commercial potential is a secondary consideration.

Hong Kong's creative economy is similar in ways to that of Tokyo, which is global metropolis in Asia. It is a capitalist economy with invisible hands at work: the government is at arm's length from the market. At present, both Japan and Hong Kong place creative industries on their current agenda, although their economies depend on finance, business, and trade. Is Cool Japan a good model to follow? Cool Japan has evolved into an administrative unit that enhances the market and promotes the operators. This approach is different from governmental initiatives that direct change and development.

The policy address "Cultural and Creative Industry," which was published in October 2009, lists six core industries in Hong Kong serving as an important impetus for Hong Kong to transition to a knowledge-based economy. A budget of HK$300 million was designated to funding CreateHK to support the creative industries in Hong Kong. Currently, the game industries are in general supported by CreateHK, which in theory promotes them. However, under the current practice, there is no direct financial support from CreateHK, nor is there any foreign promotion of games produced in Hong Kong, although research in the game industry and game exhibitions are occasionally funded. Furthermore, the role of CreateHK is more passive than that of Cool Japan. In Japan, the concept of Cool Japan was applied in the Cool Japan fund, which actively promotes creative products overseas and provides direct financial support to specific projects. At the moment, Hong Kong seems to be at the other end of the cultural policy model. While mainland China often actively promotes exports by pumping money into the industry, Hong Kong remains at a stage where CreateHK has been institutionalized but support such as export tax credits, tax rebates, and direct subsidies is absent.

In China, the problematic of cultural policy is probably due to the industry agenda in terms of game content. Censorship is the key issue. In contrast to China, the deficiency of a framework of development in Hong Kong—not necessarily the regulatory cultural policy of China—seems to be the weakest link in the Hong Kong economy.

Despite this lack of new initiatives and direct governmental support, however, some fundamental aspects of Hong Kong have always been conductive to its economy. Hong Kong has always been known for freedom of cultural expression and creation, a well-protected and free cultural market and trade, and long-established copyright laws that protect intellectual property. With or without CreateHK, these advantages could be further promoted to increase Hong Kong's competitive power in the game industry.

THE CHINA FACTOR

Hong Kong of course has weaknesses. Hong Kong's primary weakness is its small internal market compared to that of China. Thus the discourse of East Asian rivalry often requires a footnote, and this is another common public perception within the HKSAR: Hong Kong always has recourse to mainland China, and therefore, with China's huge market at its back, Hong Kong is capable of competing with Japan and South Korea. This assumption is based on the political narrative that Hong Kong needs China and is an indispensable part of China. In mediated discourse and official narratives, the Hong Kong–China collaboration is often fantasized as giving momentum to Hong Kong's future growth. And as mentioned earlier, the China and Hong Kong Closer Economic Partnership Agreement (CEPA) signed by China and Hong Kong is intended to offer benefits to various services and creative industries in Hong Kong.

However, in practice, there are restrictions in terms of implementation. Censorship was not unexpected. However, even if Hong Kong games are allowed to be sold in mainland China through the policy of CEPA, they still have to undergo the same censorship as foreign games do, which makes it difficult for Hong Kong games to enter the Chinese market. Furthermore, in China, Hong Kong game companies are still seen as "foreign game companies." The development of games in China has to be partnered with a local company, and this local company serves as a monitor. In practice, therefore, the monitoring company is a political agent that becomes a giant capitalist who takes control of the operations of the partnered companies. Hong Kong owners eventually either lose control of their company to their mainland company partner or they lose the autonomy to operate freely in the mainland market. Ultimately, they are unable to share in the profits gained in the Chinese market. Thus Hong Kong owners are reluctant to invest in the Chinese market because it is not conducive to the survival and development of Hong Kong–owned game enterprises.

Despite the CEPA, Hong Kong games produced on the mainland are not considered by the government to be games that are made in China. At the municipal level, as described in chapter 4, only the cultural clusters in Shenzhen have encouraged Hong Kong's game industry to gain a foothold in their creative hub. Thus the argument that Hong Kong would be supported by the Chinese market does not seem to apply to the game industry. The assumption that Hong Kong's creative industries might flourish under China is simply a false hope that has been promulgated by the Hong Kong government. If the HKSAR had admitted this fantasy and focused on other possibilities, the Hong Kong game industry might have explored other trajectories.

In fact, in addition to Hong Kong's relatively small game market, several infrastructural links to gaming development lag behind China. For example, in Hong Kong, the lack of well-developed online payment platforms such as China's WeChat and Alipay generally deters the flow of money in the creative industries, which are also plagued by a lack of available talent, high rental fees, and an absence of cultural clusters that support game companies. Furthermore, little venture capital has been invested in developing local games.

COLLABORATION AND COMPETITION
BEYOND EAST ASIA

The competitiveness of Hong Kong's game industries is a primary issue. Should we reminisce about the past glorious history of Hong Kong from the 1960s to the 1990s when it outran the other three "Asian dragons," South Korea, Singapore, and Taiwan? After the perceived death of Hong Kong

Cantopop (Fung & Shum, 2012; 2014) and the rise of South Korean pop in the region, is it still realistic to consider winning the cultural battle? When China has absorbed Hong Kong's cinema by coproduction, is the discourse of competition still valid? I argue that the discourse of East Asian rivalry is so predominant that few voices from Hong Kong, Japan, or South Korea are critical of competition in the East Asian region. In Hong Kong, though the competition is not a zero-sum game, there is also the practical question of Hong Kong's ability to compete in a business ecology that consists of keen competition in a well-developed and perhaps saturated game market. There might be a need to rearticulate this discourse beyond the thesis of East Asian rivalry.

Asia itself could be considered. Sze Yan Ngai, owner of Gameone, which is the only publically listed local game company in Hong Kong, estimates that the entire revenue of the game industry is US$100 billion. According to Newzoo, the revenue of the game industries in the Asia-Pacific region is now US$51.2 billion, whereas China produced another US$27.5 billion in revenue (Newzoo, 2017b). Thus, when revenue from other parts of Asia is included, US$100 billion is not an inaccurate estimate. The market in Asia is thus much bigger if we go beyond East Asia. For example, Taiwan has fourteen publicly listed game corporations, and it is one of the most game-friendly regions in East Asia. Beyond East Asia, at least one-third of the market could be expanded.

Second, it seems that Hong Kong has forgotten its history of interactions with other Asian countries. Closely connected to Hong Kong is Southeast Asia, which is a popular tourist destination for Hong Kong citizens. However, it is more than a venue for consumption. In the 1950s and 1960s, vinyl records of Hong Kong pop music were made and produced in various Southeast Asian countries such as Malaysia. Chinese communities in Vietnam, Thailand, Indonesia, and Singapore were once a huge market for Hong Kong Cantopop (Fung, 2009; Fung & Shum, 2012). Since the 1970s, Hong Kong movies and TV programs have been exported to these Southeast Asian countries although the heyday of these creative industries in Hong Kong has passed (Lii, 2005). Thus, instead of competing with "advanced" countries and assuming that these are the only competitors, Hong Kong game companies could take advantage of the cultural, linguistic, and geographic proximity of Hong Kong to Southeast Asia to develop new markets and collaborate with companies in these regions to develop games for this regional market. This move would be timely because of the recent emergence of game companies in Southeast Asia.

COLLABORATION VS. RIVALRY

The nature of the rivalry among the current East Asian countries cannot be discussed purely in terms of competitiveness. It is no longer commercial competition in a free market. Because each state can support game developers and operators and implement protective policies that prevent exports and discourage foreign companies from establishing branches, the competition has evolved into a national competition, which Yong and Downing call the "recentering" of power in the geocultural market of East Asia (2008). For the sake of increasing their soft power, South Korea and China are willing to use state resources to skew the free market. Eventually, with the success of their industries and the rise of soft power, no critical reflection will be necessary with regard to antagonistic and bellicose competition. Furthermore, would these state resources be channeled to other areas for social good or for different social groups rather than for soft power?

While this rivalry over cultural power—not military power—is legitimate and globally acceptable, a much omitted and unattended discourse includes regional collaboration, alliances, and linkages in Asia. Of course, the PRC initiated the Association of Southeast Asian Nations, the Asian Development Bank, and the Asian Infrastructural Investment Bank. However, these are high-level regional alliances for monetary purposes, and quite often, they are reduced to political or power relationships among nations. A discourse that takes into account regional partnerships among various East Asian countries, including China, in specific cultural or creative industries is rarely heard.

As we saw in chapter 5, the South Korean game industry has recently developed games in collaboration with Japanese content providers, and South Korean game corporations also depend on local Chinese publishers for game distribution. However, such joint forces among East Asian nations tend to be undermined by diplomatic disputes. There was significant media coverage of China's ban of Korean pop culture, mainly music and audiovisual products, as a protest against South Korea's installation of a Terminal High Altitude Area Defense (THAAD) missile system, although the Seoul government later showed signs of backing down (Harris, 2017). The fear of cultural invasion persists. For example, it is still illegal to broadcast Japanese pop and television dramas via land-based television in South Korea, even though South Korea ended its embargo on the import of Japanese pop, films, and games in 2004. It appears that within East Asia, cultural wars have continued since World War II. Naturally, this overshadows the fact that cultural collaboration can be symbiotic for all collaborators, and ultimately such collaboration could expand the East Asian game market. Finding a way past East Asian rivalry may be beneficial for all parties involved.

POLICY RECOMMENDATIONS
FOR HONG KONG

Finally, we return to Hong Kong. Because this book focuses on cultural policy in relation to Hong Kong, we should reevaluate recommendations that have been commonly given to the government for consideration. At present, the game industry is still the largest creative industry in Hong Kong in terms of revenue generated. According to the results of a 2017 survey on digital entertainment by CreateHK (I served as investigator for the study), there are 122 game companies in Hong Kong. Because of the scale and the market situation, the game industry in Hong Kong cannot be said to be "far behind" that of other East Asian countries. However, a cultural policy could accelerate its growth, and there is room for expansion.

If Hong Kong desires a more vibrant game scene or a much more efficiently utilized economic driver propelled by the game industry, the government must take an active, strategic role in developing the game industry. In other words, the government's strategic presence is almost a given in the international game scene. If Hong Kong attempts to perpetuate yesterday's myth of a bottom-up, market-led industry development model, it will continue to lag behind the competition in a content-based, knowledge-driven economy. I neither propose the displacement of competitors in the regional economic competition nor stress the rivalry in the East Asian region. Instead, I argue that simply reinforced by governmental support in financing, research, and promotion, for example, Hong Kong may be able to produce diverse and creative cultural content in games that highlight the characteristics of Hong Kong.

In some models of the creative industries, such as those of the EU, the creative industries are not developed with the aim of competing for soft power. Academic and industrial research on policy or technology for long-term development is an alternative. Policy makers, academics, and entrepreneurs could join in further developing the game industry. In addition to technological exploration in market research and policy research, experts and game talent from China, Korea, Japan, and other parts of the world could be invited to exchange ideas in forums, seminars, and private meetings with game developers in Hong Kong to explore possibilities of collaboration. The scope of discussion and research could be broadened to include a legal framework of virtual currency, an interactive online payment gateway, and infrastructural data-center support to facilitate transactions in the creative industries. Combined with the findings of research, these measures could reduce the commercial role of the government and address the real needs of society. International exchanges might also reduce the tension among the competitors in the region and serve to change the current scenario from one of rivalry to one of collaboration.

Talent training is rarely mentioned in cultural policies, which is one draw-back to the state-driven policies that are often initiated by the ministries or bureaus that govern the economy and education. This kind of social invest-ment is often outside the jurisdiction of such departments. I interviewed an undergraduate student who aspired to be a game programmer in South Korea. He was a science student at Yonsei University, one of the most prestigious private universities in Seoul, but he would spend an almost equal amount of time at a game-training college after his formal schooling in order to be equipped with the skills needed by game companies after he graduated. The main point is that even in an advanced game nation such as South Korea, training workers for the game industry has not been considered a part of the curriculum. In Hong Kong, despite related programs such as a master's de-gree in multimedia and entertainment technology offered by the School of Design at the Hong Kong Polytechnic University and a higher diploma in computer games and animation provided by the Hong Kong Institute of Vocational Education, the content and focus do not meet the game industry's needs. According to the owner of Gameone, around six months are required to train one programmer for the company. These findings indicate a gap between educational institutions and the game industry. Clearly, stronger links and more communication between educational institutions and the in-dustry are needed to bridge this gap and provide customized training pro-grams for the game industry. In addition, in societies such as Hong Kong, gaming has a negative image because it is perceived as disrupting familial communication, causing addiction, and encouraging self-indulgence. Thus potential talent is discouraged from working in the industry. Hence a cultural policy is required to balance consumers' interests and counteract the social harm of gaming.

Because any discourse regarding East Asian rivalry emphasizes competi-tion, the possibilities of collaboration are rarely discussed. Hong Kong is an international finance center in which legal and copyright protection and a free-market economy represent yet another strength of Hong Kong's creative industries in general. Tencent and Kingsoft, the largest game companies in China, take advantage of Hong Kong's mature investment market and are listed as public companies in Hong Kong. The incorporation of other game companies, domestic or foreign, is a way for them to expand. The robust legal framework, sound financial infrastructure, simple taxation system, and absence of currency control in Hong Kong could possibly serve to attract European and North American enterprises and to negotiate with mainland Chinese game companies. Specifically, in dealing with copyright and intel-lectual property issues, Hong Kong could serve as a neutral and credible hub inside Chinese territory for business negotiations on behalf of foreign enter-prises as well as between U.S. and European enterprises in handling copy-right disputes and violations. Moreover, Hong Kong should be ready for collaboration with game companies in Europe and North America, in addition to those in Asian countries, for the development of games and long-term distribution and publishing alliances.

HONG KONG IN COLLABORATION WITH MAINLAND CHINA

However, the question is whether Hong Kong could possibly collaborate with mainland China in the development of its game industry regardless of potential competition with Japan and South Korea. As discussed earlier, the present cultural policy does not encourage Hong Kong game companies to establish offices or develop games in China. Nonetheless, collaboration could take place at a nongovernmental level, such as among game workers and game companies. It is possible that collaboration could occur on the governmental level in the future. In recent years, Tencent has led the development of the gaming industry, but there are few comparable companies in Hong Kong.

As game industry development flourishes, large numbers of small and medium-size companies will continue to be established, resulting in high demand for talent in the mainland market and in Hong Kong. However, in Hong Kong and China, education for professionals and game industries is still lacking in curricula with regard to game planning and development, talent training, and training personnel for game industry operations and management. Newly emerging areas that address international user experience, augmented reality, virtual reality, and other special technical skills are scarce. In this regard, Hong Kong could work with different governmental units or private companies in China to provide training by professional trainers who could be invited from all over the globe. The individuals trained would be from Hong Kong, China, and Asia.

From the perspective of mainland China, when the Hong Kong–China collaborative initiative becomes a major discourse, importing and introducing Hong Kong's training model for the game industry will surely be an option. Various universities in Hong Kong could offer quality education and curricula for the creative industries with a view to providing workers for the industry both locally and on the mainland. The educational content could be codeveloped by tertiary institutions and the government, taking into the account the needs and the input of the local creative industries. In terms of the content and direction of personnel training, the education could include entire value chains of the creative industries, including games, novels, comics, animation, and films, for sustainable development and for providing synergies among all creative industries. Historically, Hong Kong has been known for its creativity. Several top Chinese online game titles such as *Demi-Gods and Semi-Evils*, *Juedai Shuangjiao* (Two Peerless Heroes), and *Fung Wan* (Wind and Cloud) are based on *wuxia* fictions that were created by the famous Hong Kong writers Jin Yong, Gu long, Ni Kuang, and Ma Wing Shing. These games are valuable intellectual property. Hong Kong's background as a creative hub for the content asset s of Hong Kong is an inherent advantage for training and pedagogy in content creation and creativity, which are much-neglected elements in the discourse of the creative industries.

In addition to cultural flow, education also affects the flow of talent and labor. Because education has become a major avenue for migration and there is an established system and admission quota in Hong Kong for mainland students, the attraction of talented students interested in the creative industries through different kinds of admission quotas could be sustained and expanded. Graduates could immigrate to Hong Kong to provide an additional workforce for the game industry, and they could also choose to return to the mainland to serve China's cultural industries. At present, the Hong Kong government's Admission Scheme for Mainland Talents and Professionals, which was designed to attract mainland labor, is restrictive and serves only as a secondary path for bringing talent to Hong Kong.

In mainland China, because most workers in the mainland game companies are generally "self-taught," the graduates returning from Hong Kong could fit the needs of the mainland's own game industry. In addition, game workers in China potentially would require a nationally recognized, professional qualification. Recently, the Communication University of China and the Beijing University of Posts and Telecommunications and other tertiary educational institutions have established colleges that provide undergraduate degrees for potential workers in the game industry.

In fact, the exorbitant increase in the number of gaming enterprises on the mainland has created a high demand for workers, hence raising the salary levels of mainland talent. The salaries of some positions exceed those in Hong Kong. An education provided in Hong Kong might in fact reverse this talent flow. It would not only solve the youth employment issue in Hong Kong but also relieve pressure on the labor market. The usual argument for the integration of Hong Kong and China in the past was economic; the flow of talent and culture—the human dimension—was often downplayed.

The sluggishness of this human flow has already led to other consequences. Because of a lack of labor and the resulting increase in labor costs, game companies have begun to outsource parts of their game production to countries in Southeast Asia, such as Vietnam and Malaysia, where there is a large workforce and salaries are much less. In my interviews with representatives of the game industries in Jiangsu and Zhejiang, they said that they subcontracted jobs to Southeast Asia to reduce costs. The provision of education in the creative industries in Hong Kong would also benefit students in those Southeast Asia countries where the game industry has gotten a foot-hold.

Nevertheless, Hong Kong's agency is limited in terms of policy making and development. The scale of Hong Kong's gaming industry is small, and Hong Kong gaming enterprise s have not reached the same level as those of mainland China. With the exception of a few (i.e., Gameone and a few Taiwanese gaming companies in Hong Kong), they mostly rely on one or two important game titles to sustain their business. Hence most Hong Kong companies have little experience in managing large-scale production teams with multiple lines of production.

Because of differences in the gaming market and its scale, although Hong Kong can learn from China, there is no need for Hong Kong to imitate the Chinese model in terms of cultural policy and the management of game enterprises. Culturally, Hong Kong has always bred a much wider variety of both ideologies and popular culture. Combined with Hong Kong's own ad-vantage in management, quality assurance, finance, and technology, the tra-jectory of the development of the game industry in Hong Kong should differ from that in mainland China.

In the gaming industry, user experience, game design, art direction, stra-tegic planning, interactive game development (for mobile games), and sys-tem construction (for Web games) are important aspects. It is worth mention-ing a few areas that are particularly pertinent to the online gaming industry in Hong Kong.

In Hong Kong, user habits and consumer experience differ from that of their counterparts in the mainland. While *wuxia* or Chinese martial arts games are equally popular in Hong Kong, which is primarily a Chinese community, perceptions of culture, wealth, economic systems, and cultural taste are different. Thus games such as *Business Tycoon*, a type of online business-strategic game, was played by white-collar workers in Hong Kong in 2010. Apparently, these players enjoyed the virtual experience of running a company, perhaps because they dreamed of owning a company in the real world. The game generated a total revenue of HK$8 million for the game company. Hence, it might be concluded that this market and game perfor-mance are resonant with the local worldview, habits, and consumer tastes of Hong Kong. The gaming experience sometimes can be replicated and some-times it cannot. It is logical for Hong Kong game companies to develop and design their own unique games.

In terms of artistic technique, direction, and design, Hong Kong games are unique. Many popular games in Hong Kong, such as *Fung Wan*, share with local comics a uniquely detailed, line-sketching style, and they appeal to local players who have grown up with this Hong Kong culture. However, when a game is developed to target a wider audience in Asia, Japanese cute or "fantasy" characters are needed. In the Chinese market, an "ink-ish" or calligraphy-like format might appeal to many gamers.

At present, China is the giant in the world's game industries. Competing with global game industries or exporting games to China is impractical for Hong Kong in terms of the number of games and the quality of games required, even if Hong Kong were to have the autonomy to operate freely in China. Simply put, the scale of Hong Kong game companies is small. In 2017, a digital entertainment survey in Hong Kong showed that the average company had only seven to ten staff members. The game companies in Hong Kong typically have no more than one hundred staff members, whereas in China, the staff of major companies work in factory-like offices. In China, most of the companies that I visited, including Tencent and Perfect World, had over one thousand staff working in gaming-related departments. In terms of input, including capital and talent, in Hong Kong the workforce is simply not large enough. Indeed, Hong Kong lacks the human resources to tackle national game promotion and marketing in Internet cafes, game exhibitions, and pop-up events. Moreover, considerable differences exist in culture, lifestyle, and habits between Hong Kong's game market and the mainland game market. Game professionals in Hong Kong in general lack a detailed understanding of consumer psychology on the mainland. In Hong Kong, the argument for taking advantage of China's market has no grounds for support. In fact, it could be said that Hong Kong's game industry is fortunate not to have been absorbed by China's game industry.

Instead, an understanding and knowledge of Chinese game companies might help reveal sources and business opportunities by which the Hong Kong game industry could benefit. This would require the conscious effort of Hong Kong academic institutions or game corporations to survey the market in China with the government's assistance or by the commissioning of a research study in China. These measures might further Hong Kong's understanding of new trends in gaming and the habits of mainland Chinese players, leading to suggestions for relevant game adjustment and localization. By negotiating and collaborating with mainland game companies, Hong Kong's game companies could publish made-in-China games locally, thus increasing their overall revenues in the market. Local game companies could localize Chinese games and respond quickly to the market, retain gamers, and maintain a relatively stable performance when they operated such Chinese games in Hong Kong. Such collaboration could benefit both Hong Kong game companies and investors and mainland game companies by earning additional revenue outside China.

In short, rather than having unrealistic expectations about depending on the Chinese market for revenue, an alliance and partnership with China's game companies—rather than competition—could augment both markets. Despite the dominance of China's game industry, a small window is now open for Hong Kong's creative talent and for Hong Kong's entrepreneurship in animation and game companies in Shenzhen. In a special project, the Shenzhen government now encourages Hong Kong's companies to operate under an experimental pilot scheme in the Qianhai area. This project is also seen as a way to strengthen Shenzhen's own competitiveness in an intense domestic Chinese market. It is expected that collaboration—in talent, game publishing, and development—could enlarge all markets not only in China but also in East Asia and beyond. This discourse is more rational and sensible than the discourse of East Asian rivalry. Capitalism accentuates and venerates competition, which was exemplified in the World Economic Forum's annual global competitiveness report (World Economic Forum, 2017). When globalization and free capitalism are under attack, there at least should be room for an alternative discourse that prioritizes global collaboration.

CULTURAL INDUSTRIES AND CREATIVITY

Research on the game industry as a creative industry has been performed not only to maximize turnover, increase exports to East Asian countries, and construct a seamless policy—as in this book—but also to decode its cultural content and to analyze the audience's interpretation. The game industry is the leading creative industry in Hong Kong, and it is a link to other creative industries such as television, comics, fiction, films, design, and other arts-related industries. This book has attempted to reveal the connection of such industries to a higher goal: the social good. The historical legacy of Hong Kong's creative industries is to continue the mission of fostering the creativity of Hong Kong cinema, extending Hong Kong's coloniality to its modernity, and recording the political changes, ideologies, and memories of Hong Kong in television drama. The study of the game industry, as well as a critical cultural policy perspective, should not deviate from the mission of knowledge contribution and the betterment of society—that is, its praxis.

To take a step back, although we have to evaluate cultural policy critically, we should be aware of the fact that cultural industries can foster social good as well as social evil. Gaming can lead to social problems—although not huge social structural problems—as discussed in chapter 2. Addiction, distraction from work, overspending on online games, and so forth are possible. In this book, these social issues are not discussed in proportion to the cultural policy considered. With regard to East Asian cultural policy, Japan is an advanced society that on one hand has administrative units that refrain from politicizing the content of games in a liberal and free economy, thereby safeguarding games and other creative industries from becoming tools for propaganda and indoctrination. On the other hand, without denying the value of the game industry in Cool Japan, many regulations have been implemented not to increase the scale of the creative industries and the number of players but to promote consumer rights, a healthier game culture, and the protection of minors. However, few studies have examined the hidden, negative effects of the cultural industries. There should be studies of the creative industries that represent the noncreative aspects and problems created by cultural policy.

After all, a distinctive characteristic of the creative industries is not their profitability; other industries might be better examples. The creativity in creative industries has been long forgotten. Few academic studies have criticized the lack of discussion of creativity in the creative economy and cultural industries. At most, creativity in the cultural industries is seen as a management issue and organizational necessity (Jeffcutt & Pratt, 2002). I argue that within the creative industries, creativity is not measured by the fluidity (number) of ideas or the originality (rarity) of ideas (Lubart, 1999). Creativity represents the diversity of ideas, content, and values that are embodied in the content produced and distributed. In Hong Kong's creative industries, the production of free, diverse, and creative content is widely recognized as the advantage of Hong Kong over China, Singapore, and other Southeast Asian countries that are shackled by various ideological, religious, and cultural constraints. The content of media products, similar to other media content, has legal protection against state-ideological control and content censorship, which continues to safeguard Hong Kong's creative industries. Hong Kong applies a classification system for print and audiovisual cultural products, enabling a diversity of game products (and other products, such as comics, films, and television) to be made available in the market for consumers of different ages. In general, in addition to game creation and development, the creation of cultural products flourishes against a background of freedom of speech and a marketplace of ideas. The bottom-up approach of a democratic cultural policy that includes the opinions and suggestions of citizens, consumers, and representatives of the game industry seems more appropriate (Gray, 2012). In line with this argument, creative industries, trade associations, universities, and research institutions should uphold this dimension of creativity in order to guarantee that the system fosters the steady creation of diversified and free content for the market in the long run. The game industry and its market industry chain should be important stakeholders and drivers.

FUTURE CHALLENGES FOR THE GAME INDUSTRY

Going forward, in Hong Kong, there is little doubt about the development of and the potential growth of the game industry. However, the future holds challenges for both Hong Kong and other East Asian nations. There will be a major reshuffle of the game industries in this region because of the popularity of mobile gaming. At present, in the global market, the revenues of mobile gaming have gradually caught up with those of online gaming. In 2017, the revenue from global mobile gaming was US$46.1 billion, which accounted for 42 percent of all global gaming industries (Newzoo, 2107a). The new mobile technology also melds game products with other types of mobile entertainment. At present, the entire industry is focusing on new mobile Internet products and applications as the next stage of revenue growth. Because games on mobile devices result in wider exposure in terms of time and daily use, the entire gaming industry is expected to grow rapidly. But because the technology involved is different and it involves a new game engine, there might be a new battle ahead .

In Hong Kong and China, the migration of the game industry to mobile gaming is expected to push the industry to reach a new zenith. Another wave of East Asian rivalry is likely to occur. Because mobile games require a shorter production cycle (one to two years compared to three to four years for online games), a smaller workforce is needed, and production costs are reduced. Although they lack the enormous strength of China's giant companies, South Korean game companies could also compete with them. Mobile games produced in Hong Kong could become global hits (e.g., *Tower of Saviors* was developed by the Hong Kong company Mad Head in 2013). Because mobile games run on Google Play in Android and iOS platforms, East Asian games can be easily accessible outside Asia, and global game companies will join the intense competition in Asia. With this influx of global capital, the current discourse of East Asian rivalry will become increasingly complex, the competition will be increasingly global, and rivalry and collaboration will take different forms.

THE IRONY OF CULTURAL POLICY

With regard to the role of cultural policy, because of its strong discourse, combined with a free capitalist market, it is expected that it will remain a vital mechanism in the cultural and creative industries. Regardless of the evidence of the efficiency and effectiveness of cultural policy, by default it should work in neoliberal markets in which regulations are designed to facilitate a free market, global flow, and minimal state interference. The neoliberal system is based on the maximization of profit for capital as long as the capitalists, who are powerful movers in the market, promote flow, logistics, and trade with capital. In theory, any policy that disturbs the market—ironically reversing the neoliberal logic—should be removed or minimized so that the neoliberal system functions with perfect efficiency. Various states, including those that celebrate free markets and capitalist markets, espouse cultural policies that ironically both interfere with and escalate production in

the creative industries. This concept is definitely newfangled if not innovative, contradictory as it seems. If cultural policy is introduced in the market,
it inexorably serves as a second force—a capitalist force—in the market.
Thus it is possible that these joint forces could accelerate the development of
the creative industries if cultural policy is introduced. Of course, how, to
what extent, and in what form such cultural policies might affect the market
would vary.

   In the case of Cool Japan, cultural policy adheres to the original capitalist
system, but cultural policy of any kind is not overly "invasive." In South
Korea, state-driven initiatives constitute a strong power that operates in tandem with capitalist power. However, South Korea's hands-off policy has
allowed construction of a significant Internet infrastructure to facilitate capitalist forces. In China, the numerous cultural clusters have become a relatively weak force compared to their direct financial subsidies. Hong Kong lacks
even minimal intervention. Hong Kong is in urgent need of essential infrastructure and support for its creative industries. For instance, because of
various restrictions on the monetary transaction system, there is no commonly available online payment platform for creative industries and e-commerce.
Without an independent online or mobile payment platform, young gamers
have to rely on their parents to pay for items and devices in games. This
situation will seriously affect the mobile game revenues of the Apple Store
and Google Play on mobile devices that require payment by credit card or
gift card. In late 2013, gift cards for Google Play were available only at
convenience stores (HK$200, HK$500, and HK$1,000). The absence of a
convenient online money transaction system hinders the spontaneous consumption of online games. In addition, in Hong Kong, the cultural clusters,
namely Science Park and Cyberport, which still operate on the logic of free
supply and demand, charge most companies the market price, and they provide only a limited number of start-ups with office space. There is no specific
support for the game industry. Although Hong Kong, Japan, and other countries might be cautious about the imposition of a strong cultural policy for the
creative industries, it seems that no parties have objected to a sound and well-
structured infrastructure for the development of the creative industries.

EPILOGUE: THE STUDY OF
CULTURAL POLICY AS A VOCATION

In this book, the perceived competition, its discourse, and the Hong Kong
game industry vis-à-vis the Chinese and the East Asian game industries have
been examined and analyzed. I would like to stress that this book presents an
informed cultural study that is largely supported by empirical data drawn
from macro statistics and personal interviews. As a social scientist, I have

attempted to organize and present the data objectively. As a cultural studies scholar, I have also attempted to append a critical angle to the data, the analysis, and the interpretation, and I have even tried to question the paradigm of cultural policy research. This does not mean that cultural policy research is not vital; on the contrary, from a layperson's point of view, it could be asked whether cultural studies are too abstract, conceptual, and theoretical. Should praxis be the way to transform society? How many people, including policy makers, are familiar with the discourse of the praxis that we have examined? In this book, I perform an experimental exploration of a fundamentally fresh approach to policy, including cultural policy. We change societies by directly and explicitly implementing policy recommendations, including those made in cultural policy. Policy makers in this sense are just pragmatic bureaucrats, not scholars of cultural studies in irony towers. To a certain extent, this approach indicates a strong need to integrate studies of applied cultural policy with the abstract perspectives of cultural studies. In the last instance, both cultural policy and cultural studies carry normative overtones that can serve to enlighten our society despite different research outcomes and perspectives.

Seeking a coherent theme throughout the book, I uphold the view that Hong Kong's creative industries and those of other nations should see collaboration as a way toward synergy between and betterment of both industry and society. The political reality may be that East Asian or global rivalry is not likely to cease but will escalate. East Asian collaboration, global unitedness, mutual sharing, and regional inclusiveness are admittedly far-off ideals, if not wishful imaginings. However, this does not mean that academic research should not intercede. Should not academics, in addition to searching for knowledge, verity, and truth in their research, undertake a mission to pursue the *good*?

Personally, as a scholar studying Hong Kong's creative industries, cultural policy, and popular culture, I recognize the dual risk of falling into compartmentalized disciplines or of researching cultural artifacts that are trivial, marginal, or outside the realms of gender, ethnicity, class, and so on. However, it is precisely such nonclassified fields, such ambiguous areas of research and down-to-earth activities, that are resonant with the everyday, ordinary-life culture that we, as scholars of culture studies (Williams, 1989), should embrace. Forty years ago, cultural studies were an unrecognized, unauthoritative field. Thus, despite the risk of nonidentity or lack of rigor, we as intellectuals should recognize our vocation to engage in the pursuit of knowledge and action to transform culture (Weber, 1946).

REFERENCES

Behrman, M. (2011). *Game development and digital growth*. Helsinki: EGDF.

Banks, J., and Keane, M. (2013). *CCI draft report on Australian and North American game industries*.

Cao, Y., and Downing, J. (2008). The realities of virtual play: Video games and their industry in China. *Media, Culture and Society, 30*(4), 515–529.

Fung, A. (Ed.). (2009). *Riding a melodic tide: The development of Cantopop in Hong Kong* [歌潮・汐韻：香港粵語流行曲的發展]. Hong Kong: Subculture Press.

Fung, A. (2016). Redefining creative labor: East Asian comparisons. In M. Curtin and K. Sanson (Eds.), *Precarious creativity* (pp. 200–214). Berkeley: University of California Press.

Fung, A., and Shum, S. [馮應謙, 沈思]. (2012). *Melodic memories: The historical development of the music industry in Hong Kong* [悠揚・憶記：香港音樂工業發展史]. Hong Kong: Subculture Press.

Fung, A., and Shum, S. [馮應謙, 沈思]. (2014). Is Hong Kong popular music dead? Or is there any new survival ecology? [香港流行音樂已死，還是有新的生存形態]. In E. Man [文潔華] (Ed.), *Hong Kong's canton culture* (pp. 24–34). [香港既廣東文化] Hong Kong: Commercial Press.

Gray, C. (2009) Managing cultural policy: Pitfalls and prospects. *Public Administration, 87*(3), 574–585.

Gray, C. (2012). Democratic cultural policy: Democratic forms and policy consequences. *International Journal of Cultural Policy, 18*(5), 505–518.

Harris, B. (2017). South Korea suspends deployment of US missile shield. *Financial Times*. Retrieved from https://www.ft.com/content/19060384-4b34-11e7-919a-1e14ce4af89b.

International Federation of the Phonographic Industry. (2016). *IFPI global music report 2016*. Retrieved from http://www.ifpi.org/news/IFPI-GLOBAL-MUSIC-REPORT-2016.

Jeffcutt, P., and Pratt, A. (2002) Managing creativity in the cultural industries. *Creativity and Innovation Management, 11*, 225–233.

Lii, D.-T. (2005). A colonized empire: Reflection of the expansion of Hong Kong movies in Asian countries. In K.-H. Chan (Ed.), *Trajectories: Inter-Asia cultural studies* (pp. 107 – 126). New York: Routledge.

Lubart, T. (1999). Creativity across cultures. In R. Sternberg (Ed.), *Handbook of creativity* (pp. 339–350). Cambridge: Cambridge University Press.

Mygaming. (2016). There are 1.8 billion gamers in the world, and PC dominates the market. Retrieved from https://mygaming.co.za/news/features/89913-there-are-1-8-billion-gamers-in-the-world-and-pc-gaming-dominates-the-market.html.

Newzoo. (2016). The global games market reaches $99.6 billon in 2016, mobile generating 33.7 percent. Retrieved from https://newzoo.com/insights/articles/global-games-market-reaches-99-6-billion-2016-mobile-generating-37/ .

Newzoo. (2017a). The global game market will reach 108.9 billion in 2017 with mobile taking 42 percent. Retrieved from https://newzoo.com/insights/articles/the-global-games-market-will-reach-108-9-billion-in-2017-with-mobile-taking-42/.

Newzoo. (2017b). The Chinese gamer 2017. Retrieved from https://newzoo.com/insights/infographics/chinese-gamer-2017/.

Nieborg, D., and de Kloet, J. (2016). A patchwork of potential: A survey of the European game industry. In A. Fung (Ed.), *Global game industry and cultural policy* (pp. 201–226). London: Palgrave Macmillan.

Statista. (2016). Film and movie industry: Statistics and facts. Retrieved from http://www.statista.com/topics/964/film/.

Weber, M. (1946). Politics as vocation. In H. H. Gerth and C. Wright-Mills (Eds.), *From Max Weber: Essays in sociology* (pp. 77–128). New York: Oxford University Press.

Williams, R. (1989). Culture is ordinary. In R. Gable (Ed.), *Resources of hope: Culture, democracy, socialism* (pp. 3–14). London: Verso.

World Economic Forum. (2017). *The global competitiveness report 2016–2017*. Retrieved from https://www.weforum.org/reports/the-global-competitiveness-report-2016-2017-1.

Index

www.ingramcontent.com/pod-product-compliance
Lightning Source LLC
Chambersburg PA
CBHW021819270326
41932CB00007B/258